English 365

Teacher's Book 1

CAMBRIDGE Professional English

English 365

Teacher's Book 1

Bob Dignen Steve Flinders Simon Sweeney

PUBLISHED BY THE PRESS SYNDICATE OF THE UNIVERSITY OF CAMBRIDGE
The Pitt Building, Trumpington Street, Cambridge, United Kingdom

CAMBRIDGE UNIVERSITY PRESS
The Edinburgh Building, Cambridge CB2 2RU, UK
40 West 20th Street, New York, NY 10011-4211, USA
477 Williamstown Road, Port Melbourne, VIC 3207, Australia
Ruiz de Alarcón 13, 28014 Madrid, Spain
Dock House, The Waterfront, Cape Town 8001, South Africa

http://www.cambridge.org
http://www.cambridge.org/elt/english365

© Cambridge University Press 2004

It is normally necessary for written permission for copying to be obtained in advance from the publisher. The Extra classroom activities and Better learning activities at the back of this book are designed to be copied and distributed in class. The normal requirements are waived here and it is not necessary to write to Cambridge University Press for permission for an individual teacher to make copies for use within his or her own classroom. Only those pages which carry the wording '© Cambridge University Press' may be copied.

First published 2004

Printed in the United Kingdom at the University Press, Cambridge

Typeface Swift *System* QuarkXpress® [HMCL]

A catalogue record for this book is available from the British Library

ISBN 0 521 75363 5 Teacher's Book 1
ISBN 0 521 75362 7 Student's Book 1
ISBN 0 521 75364 3 Personal Study Book 1 with Audio CD
ISBN 0 521 75365 1 Student's Book 1 Audio Cassette Set
ISBN 0 521 75366 X Student's Book 1 Audio CD Set

Thanks and acknowledgements

The authors would like to thank:

- Bonnie Bernström, Sally Searby, Jihad Hinawi, Martina Hruba, Jochen Lohmeyer, Anneli Ejnestrand, Chiara Nesler, Margita Westring, Montse Benet, Stein Idar Stokke, Ellen Zlotnick, Ablaziz Esseid, Paul Munden (National Association of Writers in Education, UK), Ben Ashcroft, Alison Collings, Roisin Vaughan, Polly Markandya (www.msf.org), Jürgen Robbert, Riggert Andersson, Paula Morris, Wendy Fogarty (www.slowfood.com), John Duncan, Bob Hands, Isabelle Segura, Jackie and Phil Black (Tower Street Pantry, York, UK), Tashi Ugyen, Anthony Allen (www.sroauk.org.uk), Mike Tabrett, Frank Hatke, Gayle Martz, Sarah Schechter and the students of Anglia Polytechnic University, and the students and teachers of Eurocentre, Cambridge for their help with interviews;
- the interviewees for their photographs;
- Ian Chitty, Graham Ditchfield, Eryl Griffiths, Robert Highton, Bernie Hayden, Jackie Mann, Francis O'Hara, Duncan Nicholson, Chaz Pugliese and Elizabetta Trebar for reviewing the material in its early stages;
- Mike Barker of the Norwegian Workers' Educational Association for the idea behind Define principles (page 13);
- Will Capel and Sally Searby of Cambridge University Press for their unflinching support from start to finish;
- Alison Silver for her eagle eye for detail, for her good sense and good cheer throughout the editorial and proofreading process;
- Hilary Fletcher for the picture research and Ruth Carim for proofreading;
- James Richardson for producing the recordings at Studio AVP, London;
- Hart McLeod for the design and page make-up;
- Sue Evans; Lorenza, Mathieu, Jérôme and Michael Flinders; and Lyn, Jude, Ruth and Neil Sweeney for their patience;
- colleagues and friends at York Associates and in the School of Management, Community and Communication at York St John College for their tolerance of authorial distraction;
- Chris Capper of Cambridge University Press for his immeasurable contribution to the project. It is, above all, his huge efforts which have made this book possible.

The authors and publisher would like to thank the following for permission to reproduce copyright material:

p.45 Médecins Sans Frontières, Plan and WWF (formerly known as the World Wildlife Fund) for the texts adapted from their websites (www.msf.org, www.plan-uk.org, www.panda.org), the Oxfam text is adapted from the Oxfam International website, www.oxfam.org/eng/about.htm (Oxfam GB, 274 Banbury Road, Oxford, OX2 7DZ www.oxfam.org); p.71 the article about T'ai Chi is reproduced with kind permission of Ron Perfetti www.ronperfetti.com.

Contents

Thanks and acknowledgements   5

Student's Book Contents   8

1 Introduction to *English365* Book 1   11
Welcome   11
Course components   12
Organisation of the Student's Book   12
Starting up the course   13

2 Introduction to the Teacher's Book   15
Getting ready   15
Common elements   17
Teaching type 1 units   18
Teaching type 2 units   18
Teaching type 3 units   19

3 Teacher's notes: Units 1–30   20
1 Nice to meet you   20
2 Helping people to learn   22
3 Have a good weekend   24
4 North and south   26
5 Health care – public or private?   28
6 Downtown Barcelona   30
7 Changing workspace   32
8 The A Team   34
9 I love Chicago   36
10 Eating around the world   37
11 Nice work   39
12 Do you salsa?   41
13 Chanel   42
14 Médecins Sans Frontières   45
15 Trekking in Nepal   47
Revision 1 Units 1–15   48
16 Project Stockholm   49
17 Workplace communication   51
18 Slow food   53
19 Living in Hong Kong   55
20 Online   57
21 Beirut Intercontinental   59
22 Working for Rolls Royce   61
23 Start up   62
24 I buy money   64
25 Driving to Romania   66
26 Out of order   68
27 Teaching T'ai Chi   70
28 Perfect planning   72
29 A changing world   74
30 Jets and pets   75
Revision 2 Units 16–30   77

4 Extra classroom activities   78
Teacher's notes   78
1 Who am I?   83
2 Me and my organisation   84
3 A perfect weekend   85
4 Daily routines   86
5 Alphabet soup   87
6 The place where I live   88
7 My workplace   89
8 My ideal manager   90
9 London and New York   91
10 Big or small?   92
11 Job satisfaction   93
12 Sports quiz   94
13 Life stories   95
14 The merger   96

15 Holiday home	97	**5 Better learning activities**	113
16 What are they doing?	98	Teacher's notes	113
17 Workplace communication	99	**1** Why do you want to learn English?	116
18 National dishes	100	**2** Your language learning background	117
19 Cultural rules and recommendations	101	**3** Your level	118
20 Computers in your life	102	**4** Fixing targets	119
21 Dream hotel	103	**5** Making a plan	120
22 Number work	104	**6** What makes a good language learner?	121
23 It's my business	105	**7** Learning to speak	122
24 Shopping lists	106	**8** Learning to read	123
25 A busy schedule	107	**9** Learning to listen	124
26 Problems at work	108	**10** Learning vocabulary	125
27 New Year resolutions	109		
28 Executive star	110	Teacher's diary	127
29 Forecasting the future	111		
30 Lifestyles	112		

Student's Book Contents

1 Nice to meet you
Listening
Say who you are
Grammar
The present simple 1
Pronunciation
Reply questions
Speaking
Meeting people

4 North and south
Listening
A working day in the north ... and in the south of Europe
Grammar
The present simple 2
Pronunciation
The present simple third person
Speaking
Work routines

7 Changing workspace
Listening
This is where I work
Grammar
There is/are ...
Countable and uncountable nouns
Some and any; a lot of
Pronunciation
Linking
Speaking
Where you work

10 Eating around the world
Listening
Favourite food
Grammar
Comparative and superlative adjectives
Pronunciation
Weak stress 1
Speaking
Comparing

13 Chanel
Listening
Gabrielle (Coco) Chanel – inventor of the fashion industry
Grammar
The past simple
Pronunciation
Past simple verbs
Speaking
Your life and background

2 Helping people to learn
Reading
A new future
Vocabulary
Job responsibilities
Speaking
Your job
Communicating at work
Telephoning 1: Getting information

5 Health care – public or private?
Reading
Working at Växjö hospital
Vocabulary
People and organisations
Speaking
Introducing your organisation
Communicating at work
Telephoning 2: Taking messages

8 The A team
Reading
We're a great team
Vocabulary
Describing people at work
Speaking
The people you work with
Communicating at work
Meeting a visitor at the airport

11 Nice work
Reading
Homeworking
Vocabulary
Work
Speaking
What you want from your job
Communicating at work
Emails 1: Giving your emails a clear structure

14 Médecins Sans Frontières
Reading
Médecins Sans Frontières – working to help people
Vocabulary
Organisational structure
Speaking
Your organisation
Communicating at work
Welcoming visitors to your organisation

3 Have a good weekend
Social phrases
At the office
Listening
Enjoying your weekend
Vocabulary
Your free time
Speaking
Weekends

6 Downtown Barcelona
Social phrases
Shopping
Listening
A shoppers' paradise
Vocabulary
Location and shopping
Speaking
Where you live

9 I love Chicago
Social phrases
Getting around
Listening
It's my kind of town
Vocabulary
City life
Speaking
Where you live

12 Do you salsa?
Social phrases
Responding to news
Listening
I hate watching TV
Vocabulary
Verbs and nouns for sport and physical activities
Speaking
Sport and physical exercise

15 Trekking in Nepal
Social phrases
Air travel
Listening
Walking at 5,000 metres
Vocabulary
Holidays and travel
Speaking
Holidays

Revision 1 Units 1–15

16 Project Stockholm
Listening
What project are you working on at the moment?
Grammar
The present continuous 1
Pronunciation
Sentence stress
Speaking
Describing temporary situations

19 Living in Hong Kong
Listening
Chinese culture
Grammar
Should and *have to*
Pronunciation
Word stress
Speaking
Organising a visit to another country

22 Working for Rolls Royce
Listening
Work is like a second home
Grammar
Many, much, a few, a little
Pronunciation
Saying numbers and prices
Speaking
Numbers and quantity

25 Driving to Romania
Listening
A job everyone wants to do
Grammar
The present continuous 2
Pronunciation
Weak stress 2
Speaking
Future plans

28 Perfect planning
Listening
Have you organised everything?
Grammar
The present perfect
Pronunciation
Spelling and pronunciation
Speaking
Organising things at work / Making small talk

17 Workplace communication
Reading
Communication of the future
Vocabulary
Communication verbs
Speaking
Managerial qualities
Communicating at work
Emails 2: Replying to emails

20 Online
Reading
Computer heaven or hell?
Vocabulary
Computers and the Internet
Speaking
People and their computers
Communicating at work
Telephoning 3: Arranging meetings

23 Start up
Reading
Managing a small business
Vocabulary
Money and business finance
Speaking
Solving a business problem
Communicating at work
Helping visitors

26 Out of order
Reading
Problems in Pennsylvania
Vocabulary
Words and expressions for problem solving
Speaking
Solving work problems
Communicating at work
Telephoning 4: Solving problems by phone

29 A changing world
Reading
A year in Germany
Vocabulary
Describing change
Speaking
Change
Communicating at work
Emails 3: Arranging meetings by email

18 Slow food
Social phrases
At the restaurant
Listening
A great place to eat
Vocabulary
Food and drink
Speaking
Eating out

21 Beirut Intercontinental
Social phrases
Staying in a hotel
Listening
It's a great place to stay
Vocabulary
Hotels and hotel service
Speaking
Hotels

24 I buy money
Social phrases
Money talk
Listening
Hey, big spender
Vocabulary
Money and shopping
Speaking
Spending

27 Teaching T'ai Chi
Social phrases
Inviting
Listening
T'ai Chi can improve your life
Vocabulary
Health
Speaking
Decision making

30 Jets and pets
Social phrases
Saying goodbye
Listening
Working with animals
Vocabulary
Learning for life
Speaking
Continuing your learning

Revision 2 Units 16–30

File cards
Grammar reference
Tapescripts
Answer key

1 Introduction to *English365* Book 1

Welcome

Who is *English365* for?
This course is for working adults who want English for their working and personal lives. Student's using Book 1:
- are at post-elementary to lower-intermediate level
- may have studied English in the past but need a new extensive course to refresh, practise and consolidate what they know as well as to learn new language
- need a supportive environment to build speaking skills by activating known language, which is largely passive at the moment, and by learning new language and communication skills.

How long is the course?
This book provides at least 60 hours of classroom teaching. The Student's Book contains:
- 30 units which each provide 90 minutes of classroom teaching material per lesson (45 hours)
- two revision units with up to 60 minutes of extra classroom or self-study exercises to work on (2 hours).

The Teacher's Book provides an extra classroom activity linked to each unit, plus ten activities to develop students' learning strategies. Each activity takes at least 15 minutes to complete and some of them can occupy 30 minutes or more (10–20 hours).

What does *English365* give to the learner?
The course aims to provide:
- a balance between English for work, travel and leisure
- a balance between grammar, vocabulary, pronunciation and professional communication skills (at this level: writing, telephoning and dealing with visitors)
- a balance between the skills of speaking, listening, reading and writing
- clear and relevant learning aims in every unit
- stimulating content and activities to motivate adult learners
- sensitive support to students who have problems achieving the transition from passive to active use of English
- a strong emphasis on recycling and consolidation
- motivation to students to achieve a useful balance between classroom and self-study.

What about exams?
English365 Book 1 aims to take post-elementary students (Common European Framework Waystage level A2 / ALTE level 1) up to lower-intermediate level (Common European Framework Threshold level B1 / ALTE level 2). *English365* Book 2 aims to take learners through level B1 and towards intermediate level (Common European Framework Vantage level B2 / ALTE level 3). So by the time they complete *English365* Book 2, students should be ready to sit:
- the Cambridge Examinations Preliminary Business English Certificate (BEC1)
- the Cambridge Examinations Preliminary Certificate in English Language Skills (CELS1).

English365 Book 3 aims to take intermediate learners through level B2. So by the time they complete Book 3, students should be ready to sit:
- the Cambridge Examinations Vantage Business English Certificate (BEC2)
- the Cambridge Examinations Vantage Certificate in English Language Skills (CELS2).

How is it different?
1 **Authenticity** Much of the material is based on authentic interviews with real working people, many of them doing similar jobs and with similar personal and professional concerns as the people likely to be studying the book. Each unit focuses in part on a professional individual who provides the context for the subject matter. The original interviews have been converted into simplified texts for reading or rerecorded to make listening comprehension easier, but the reading and listening texts still retain the original flavour which we believe will be motivating and involving for your students.
2 **Organisation** The units are divided into three types (see Organisation of the Student's Book on page 12). We think that working through cycles of three units provides the right balance between learners' dual need for variety and for a sense of security.
3 **Vocabulary** The book has an ambitious lexical syllabus: we believe students can learn vocabulary successfully if exposed to it in the right way and that vocabulary is an important key to better understanding, better communication, progress and motivation.
4 **Grammar** The book's approach to grammar is based less on traditional PPP (Presentation – Practice – Production) and more on TTT (Teach – Test – Teach). We think that the majority of adult students at this level have been subjected to the grammar features of our syllabus through PPP already; they do need to revise and extend their existing knowledge but they don't want to be bored going through traditional presentations all over again.
5 **Self-study**
   - The Teacher's notes for each unit offer suggestions to pass on to students about how they can consolidate their classroom learning.
   - The Personal Study Book with Audio CD provides students with 15 to 30 minutes' worth of self-study material per unit and up to 15 minutes of listening material (recyclable) for each unit with a listening component.

6 **Learner training** Additional activities in the Teacher's Book, as well as the Teacher's notes to the units in the Student's Book, encourage teachers and learners to focus on the learning process itself.

Course components

There are six components for this level:
1 Student's Book
2 Classroom Audio Cassettes/CDs
3 Personal Study Book
4 Personal Study CD
5 Teacher's Book
6 website.

The **Student's Book** contains:
- an introduction to the student
- 30 classroom units plus two revision units
- file cards for pair and groupwork exercises
- a grammar reference section
- a tapescript of the Classroom Audio Cassettes/CDs
- the answer key to the exercises.

The **Classroom Audio Cassettes/CDs** contain:
- all the tracks relating to listening work in the Student's Book.

The **Teacher's Book** provides:
- an introduction to the course and how to work with it
- detailed notes on the units in the Student's Book
- 30 extra photocopiable classroom activities, each one linked to a unit in the Student's Book, supported by Teacher's notes
- 10 extra photocopiable activities for better learning, designed to improve the effectiveness of students' learning, also supported by Teacher's notes

The **Personal Study Book** contains:
- Language for language learning – an alphabetical list of all the grammatical and other terms used in the Student's Book together with definitions taken from the *Cambridge Learner's Dictionary*
- one page of self-study exercises per unit of the Student's Book for additional practice
- the answer key to the exercises
- a tapescript of the contents of the Personal Study CD.

The **Personal Study CD** contains:
- self-study listening exercises. These encourage students to practise basics like the alphabet, numbers, dates and times, etc. and are designed as remedial support for learners at this level who, we believe, often need to do consolidation work in these areas.
- the listening material relating to pronunciation work in the Student's Book (type 1 units)
- the social English dialogues in the Student's Book (type 3 units).

The **website** provides:
- information about the course
- information about the authors
- extra resources for students and teachers.

See www.cambridge.org/elt/english365

Organisation of the Student's Book

The Student's Book has 30 units plus two revision units. The 30 units are clustered into ten groups of three, over which a full range of language items and communication elements are presented and practised.

Whilst the units are designed to be delivered sequentially, their flexibility is such that they may be dealt with out of sequence if a specific need or occasion arises.

Each type of unit is designed as follows. All units contain a section called 'It's time to talk' which provides opportunities for transfer and freer practice of the main learning points. See page 18 for teaching approaches to each type of unit.

Type 1 units (Units 1, 4, 7, 10, 13, 16, 19, 22, 25 and 28)
Type 1 units present and practise:
- Listening on a work-related theme
- Grammar
- Pronunciation
- Speaking.

Rationale
Type 1 units present and practise a grammar point, introduced first through the medium of a listening exercise. The theme is work-related and the listening text also permits the passive presentation of useful vocabulary. The grammar point is then formally presented and practised and there is also extrapolation to presentation and practice of a discrete pronunciation point. The unit finishes with a supported but freer speaking practice activity which enables students to gain fluency and confidence with the grammar, whilst expressing their ideas on relevant work-related topics.

Type 2 units (Units 2, 5, 8, 11, 14, 17, 20, 23, 26 and 29)
Type 2 units present and practise:
- Reading on a work-related theme
- Work-related vocabulary
- Speaking
- Professional communication skills.

Rationale
Every second unit in the cluster presents professional vocabulary through the medium of a reading text on a work-related theme. Students develop reading skills like skimming and scanning and also have the opportunity (in 'What do you think?') to briefly discuss the issues raised in the text. There is explicit presentation and practice of vocabulary followed by a short fluency activity designed to enable students to use the vocabulary in freer and realistic exchanges. The unit finishes with a focus on professional communication, with presentation and practice of key phrases and skills. These are often introduced by means of a short listening text. The professional communication skills targeted in *English365* Book 1 are:
- telephoning
- writing emails
- basic language for welcoming and dealing with visitors.

Type 3 units (Units 3, 6, 9, 12, 15, 18, 21, 24, 27 and 30)
Type 3 units present and practise:
- Social phrases
- Listening on a general theme
- General vocabulary
- Speaking.

Rationale

Every third unit in the cluster begins with a focus on social English. Students listen to a series of short dialogues presenting language for a range of everyday situations. The listening is followed by practice exercises. The second part of each unit focuses on the presentation and practice of general vocabulary, introduced via a listening exercise. The unit finishes with a speaking activity designed to practise the vocabulary and to foster fluency and confidence when speaking about general topics.

Revision units

There are two revision units in the Student's Book, one following Unit 15 and the other after Unit 30. These contain exercises summarising the work covered thus far. They can be used in a variety of ways, including:
- to test students' knowledge
- as supplementary classroom material
- as supplementary self-study material.

Starting up the course

This section suggests different approaches to starting up a new course with *English365*. The first lesson of a new course is obviously important and can be handled in many different ways. Your aim should be not just to teach the language of Unit 1 but to create a positive attitude towards learning English in general in the mind of each student and to create a good group dynamic which will help this learning to take place. You want students to leave the lesson believing that this course is going to be:
- comprehensible
- coherent
- useful and
- enjoyable – or even fun!

Think about how you can achieve these goals. You should choose the way that you and (as far as you can anticipate this) your students feel most comfortable with. You may know everyone in your group very well or you may never have met them. They may know each other, they may not. However, you should know something about them so, as you prepare, think about the best way to start up. Once you have told them what you plan to do in this lesson, there are many possibilities. You can't take up all of the suggestions which follow but doing one or two for five to ten minutes at the start of the lesson may help to tailor the book to your style and the style of your group.

Talk to your students

Tell them that you are going to talk to them for a few minutes so that all they have to do is relax and listen. Speaking slowly and clearly, and using simple language, introduce yourself and tell your students a few things about yourself. You might introduce yourself to each student in turn. Talking to students at the beginning of a course in language they can understand (this is your challenge!) can help them relax and attune their ears to the sounds and meanings of English. Remember that they will be nervous too – some of them very much so. Use this approach to show them that you don't want them to feel under too much pressure to produce language straightaway.

Tell them how you work

You may also wish to talk about how *you* like to work, what your objectives are, and about creating a winning team, the members of which will work together to achieve individual and group objectives. Working together will give better results for everyone.

Talk about the book

Give students the chance to look through their copies of *English365* Book 1 – to see how long each unit is, how many units there are, to find the grammar reference, etc. at the back of the book, and so on. The book is a prime learning tool for them. It's important for them to be able to find their way around and have an idea of its organisational principles. In particular, point out to them the colour coding for the three different types of unit and explain briefly what these are. Tell them too about the other components, and show them in particular a copy of the Personal Study Book and accompanying CD.

Do a needs analysis

Unless you have already had the chance to do so with the students themselves, do a needs analysis of the expectations and objectives of the group or of the learning backgrounds of the learners either at the beginning of this lesson or later on. You can use any or all of the first three of the Better learning activities to support this (see page 113). Unless you have received detailed briefing on your students, you will need to find out all this information in any case during the first two or three lessons.

Do the admin

You may have administrative business to get out of the way: registers to take, attendance sheets to get signed, etc. Decide when in the lesson you want to do this.

Define principles

Get students to agree to a set of class rules for the course. For example:
- We will help each other to speak better English.
- We will not speak our own language in the classroom.

Check metalanguage

Metalanguage or classroom language (the language you or the book use to give instructions, talk about language, etc.) can be a problem and you may want to introduce or check some words in English which are important to successful classroom communication and management at this stage. You can do this progressively (see below) or you can use the Language for language learning section in the Personal Study Book.

Break the ice
Use your own ice-breaking technique for starting up with a new group of low level learners. The main content of the unit will then consolidate what you have already done. You may want to do this in the Warm up (see page 17).

If you don't have a favourite ice-breaking activity, try the following, when (some of) the students know each other, but you don't know them:

Take one victim in turn (who must remain silent) and ask the others what they know about him or her. At the end of each round of the class, you can summarise the information and the victim can say if each detail is true or not. Keep it simple by suggesting sentences like:
- Max works for IBM.
- Eva has a dog.
- Santi has four children.
- Margot lives in Madrid.

Dive in
You may prefer to go straight into the unit: it is about introducing yourself and getting to know people, so is very appropriate material for a first lesson.

And remember
Don't try all of these! Choose the one or two which you feel are most appropriate to your teaching style and to the group, as far as you can tell.

2 Introduction to the Teacher's Book

Getting ready

The language of the Teacher's notes
The 30 sets of notes in the next section are intended to provide you with ideas and support if you need them. They are not prescriptive. They are designed to enhance, not cramp your own teaching style. The imperative style (as in 'Ask', 'Check', 'Tell', etc.) is therefore only to keep the notes short and simple, not to tell you how best to do something. The less imperative style 'You could also . . .', 'You may like to . . .' signals additional ideas not directly found in the Student's Book.

Talking to students
How can you talk to students at this level so that they can understand you? It is worth repeating that when we speak to our students, we should remember to:
- speak slowly and clearly
- use vocabulary and structures (most of which) they can understand
- as far as possible, use intonation and pronunciation patterns which replicate speech at normal speed. So, for example, try to keep unstressed words and syllables unstressed even when you are speaking more slowly than usual.

It's your responsibility to make sure students understand what you say. On the other hand, it is possible to communicate a great deal to and with quite low level speakers by observing these principles; and it is also possible for students to communicate a great deal to you and to each other. One characteristic of good language learners is the extent to which they can make a little language go a long way. You can help them maximise the usefulness of what language they already possess.

From passive to active
Teachers disagree about whether lower level students should be thrown in at the deep end at the beginning of a lesson or a course by being asked to produce language straightaway, or whether they should be allowed time to get used to the language and build confidence before having big demands made on them. Both schools of thought are right – about different students. The design of these units tries to take both possibilities into account. More confident students are given opportunities to talk from the Warm up right at the start. On the other hand, more hesitant students can focus on the objectives at this stage without having to say very much.

Classroom language
It is important to check that students understand the metalanguage in the book and the instructions you give them. The load to check can be quite heavy in the early units but will dwindle away to zero as you progress through the book and repeatedly use the same terms. A list of words to check appears in every unit of Teacher's notes. A complete list of all the terms also appears in the Personal Study Book with space for students to write the translation into their own language. Encourage students to do this. Some students may know most if not all of these words but it is important to be sensitive to the possibility that some will not.

Classroom resources
The range of resources and equipment available to teachers ranges from the rudimentary, or worse, to the very sophisticated. If equipment is not so good, remember that in any case your best resources are your students and yourself.

Dictionaries
Students are recommended to buy a good learner's dictionary. The *Cambridge Learner's Dictionary* is excellent. Dictionaries are not essential in the classroom but they are helpful, and students will benefit from access to them both for classroom work and for self-study. Occasionally they can be especially useful, for example for the pronunciation work in Unit 19. If students don't have their own dictionaries, it helps to have one or two available for them in class.

The whiteboard
The Teacher's notes often recommend you to use the whiteboard to build up sets of vocabulary and collocations during a lesson both to develop students' vocabulary and also because it's good for students' morale when they can see how many words they can recognise and use.

The electronic whiteboard
One of the supreme advantages of these is that you can transfer what you have written on the board directly into a digital file on a computer instead of copying down everything you wrote up at the end of a lesson.

The overhead projector
OHPs are especially useful for pairs reporting back work in writing after a pairwork activity. They can write directly onto a transparency and then show other students the results. If you write your feedback – for example for a pairwork activity – on a transparency, you can also project it straightaway to the whole group.

Computers
Computers are especially useful for writing in the classroom. Whether you have time to provide individual correction for all your students' work outside class time is another issue!

Doing written exercises and checking answers
Written exercises can be approached in a number of different ways and you should try to vary what you ask students to do. Be attentive to their mood and level of concentration. They may welcome the opportunity to do two or three exercises alone in order to assimilate input thus far in the lesson and take a rest from the requirements of active

language manipulation and production. In this case, give them time to do one or more exercises on their own (although don't always wait for the last student to finish before moving on). Then check the answers by going round the class. However, you don't always have to say immediately whether the answer given is correct or not. Write a suggestion up on the board and ask the others to reach agreement on whether it is right or not; or ask students to lead this part of the lesson; or ask students to work in pairs. In other words, exercises and checking can be carried out more or less passively or quite actively, depending on your and their mood and needs.

Pair and groupwork

Introduction

Pairwork is an opportunity not just for practice but also for students to develop support for each other and, potentially, for them to learn from each other in terms of language competence and learning style. Encourage students to work with different partners from lesson to lesson and within lessons.

Timing

Timing is important in pair and groupwork activities, especially more open ones as in 'It's time to talk' sections. Decide how much time you want to spend on the activity. In many cases, ten minutes is plenty. If you remember that feedback will also take at least five minutes and students performing for their colleagues another five, you can see that without careful time management, too much of the lesson will be taken up in this way.

Procedure

A basic procedure for pairwork is as follows:
1 Present the activity and read through the relevant input to check understanding. Pre-teach difficult vocabulary and provide any grammatical or other models which you would like students to use.
2 Choose – or ask students to choose – pairs. If you have an odd number, work with the odd person yourself, or make a group of three.
3 If there is a preparation phase before the activity, decide whether to put some or all of the Student As and Bs together in separate groups or whether preparation should be done alone; or ask students to decide.
4 During the activity itself, walk round and monitor activity. Make notes of good and not so good language. You can write good language on the board even while the activity is still going on. You may also like to make notes directly onto a transparency to save time later.
5 You may wish students to reverse roles later. Watch the time so that both get an equal chance in both roles.
6 After the activity itself, students usually report back. The form of this will depend on the nature of the activity. You may want to summarise the findings on a problem or question for the class as a whole (or ask students to do so) – this is sometimes referred to in the Teacher's notes as doing a survey. For example, how many of them live in the town and how many in the country, how many travel by bus to work, how many by train, and by car, etc. If students were set to solve a problem, find out which solution was preferred and why. This may lead to more general discussion, so be conscious of the time available.
7 You may often invite selected pairs to perform the same activity in front of the others; or you may invite a new pair to do so. Encourage others to provide constructive criticism of these performances.
8 As the first stage in the debriefing, ask students what language or communication difficulties they had.
9 You will then provide feedback on the activity as a whole (see the section on feedback on page 17). Be conscious of the balance between feedback on the language and communication aspects of the activity.
10 Summarise the main points you want students to take away with them. Encourage them to write them down or make some other effort to retain them.
11 Ask students to assess the usefulness of the activity – in other words, for their feedback.

Serial pairwork

The non-alcoholic cocktail party is a variation on basic pairwork except that students talk to two or three others in turn during the activity. You should certainly encourage students to get up and walk around for this: getting students up and about now and again is good for their energy levels and good for kinaesthetic learners – ones who like moving about, touching and handling things, and physical activity. They will need to have pen and paper – usually a photocopy of the activity – to note down the answers to their questions. Timing is again important here because you may need to tell them when partners should swap from asking to answering questions, and when students should swap partners each time. So keep a check on your watch, and be strict.

Telephone pairwork

For pairwork on the telephone, you can suggest that students sit back-to-back, if you don't have telephone equipment for them all.

Groupwork

The Student's Book and Teacher's notes generally refer to pairwork, but you can vary things by putting students into groups of three and four. You can also put students into pairs and nominate one or two others as observers. One can provide feedback to the group, the other can provide language feedback to the pair after they have finished.

File cards

If a lesson involves using the file cards at the back of the Student's Book, you should read the roles in advance so that you have a clear idea of what students will be required to do. Most of the activities involving file cards are pairwork activities, but note that in Unit 10, for example, students work in groups of three, each with their own brief.

Students will often need time to prepare questions for their partner. Either there is specific guidance on what questions to ask or they can prepare questions on the basis of the information on their own file cards. Once again, you could decide to put all the As together in one group and all the Bs in another at this stage.

Feedback and correction
In addition to all of the above:
- Be selective. Identify the main points you want to make.
- Be positive. Give feedback on good language as well as the not so good.
- Be constructive. Praise students for their efforts before suggesting ways of doing it better.
- Get them to be constructive with each other. This is part of building a team which will help all its members to achieve more. Create an environment of mutual support.

Self-study, consolidating learning and making progress
Students are more likely to make progress if you build lots of recycling into the course and encourage students to work on their English outside the classroom. There are a variety of suggestions about how to achieve this in this book. In sum, we recommend you to:
1. revise the previous lesson of the same type at the start of every class
2. clearly state lesson objectives and remind students of these at the end of every lesson
3. make regular use of the Better learning activities in class.

We recommend you to encourage students to:
1. reread the unit in the Student's Book which they have just done with you
2. do self-study exercises for the equivalent unit in the Personal Study Book and, where applicable, to use the Personal Study Audio CD
3. do follow-up activities suggested in the Teacher's notes for each unit
4. start and maintain vocabulary notebooks
5. keep learner diaries (in English or in their own language).

Teacher's diary
The Teacher's diary at the back of this book aims to help you in your own professional development. We suggest that you make multiple photocopies of it and put the copies in a separate file. The page is self-explanatory. It is designed – realistically we hope for busy teachers – for you to spend three minutes completing one sheet for every lesson. By getting into the habit of doing this and reflecting on what you do, we hope it will encourage you to experiment, develop and communicate with other teachers about the issues which interest and involve you.

Creating a dynamic group
Last, but perhaps most importantly, aim to help create a lively, energised group of learners, a group which is ready to:
- get up and walk round to refocus when concentration dips
- offer support and positive criticism to all its members
- openly discuss language without fear of losing face
- take the initiative to lead the class.

Common elements
This section offers guidance on how to handle the lesson stages which are common to every unit.

Why are we doing this?
Always make clear what the objectives of each lesson are. At the start of every lesson:
- Explain which type of unit you are working on today.
- Then tell students the objectives of this lesson (see On the agenda).
- Identify the main points and write up key words on the board or OHP (see Teacher's notes for each unit).
- Leave them there through the lesson so that students have a clear idea of the basic structure of the lesson and also of where they are at any particular stage.

Thinking about what you are doing and where you are going helps consolidate learning.

Warm up
As the name suggests, this is intended as a quick way into the unit, to help you and the students focus on the main objectives and to get them used to speaking the language. Particularly at this level, students need time to warm up. The Warm up is intended as a short activity involving looking at the picture of the unit personality, answering or briefly discussing one or two questions, doing a simple matching exercise, etc. Do not let the Warm up go on for too long. There will be opportunities to discuss related questions in a more open-ended way later in the lesson.

It's time to talk
This is the open practice section of each unit, designed to consolidate the learning which you are aiming for learners to achieve within a relevant and useful context: a transfer from closed to open and from a generic to a more specific contextualisation, although this varies from unit to unit. See also notes on pair and groupwork above.

Remember
Check this section quickly with the whole class. Then ask:

What did we do today?
If necessary, remind students of the objectives of this lesson (by referring to your key lesson structure words on the board or On the agenda).

Follow up
For you: use the Extra (photocopiable) classroom activity in this book which corresponds to the unit you are teaching.
For students: encourage students to consolidate their learning by doing regular homework and self-study between lessons. This will make all the difference to the amount of progress many of them make. Standard ways to do this are:
1. to reread the unit in the Student's Book
2. to read the corresponding unit in the Personal Study Book and do the exercises.

See the Teacher's notes for each unit for other suggestions.

Timing
The timings suggested in the following sections are based on a 90-minute lesson. They are intended to provide broad guidance only. Your timings will obviously depend enormously on the specific lesson, the kind of class you have and the kind of teacher you are. Be flexible. Don't allow too much planning to get between you and the students. Over-rigidity can stop you listening to your students and can destroy real communication.

Teaching type 1 units

Unit structure and timing

The structure of type 1 units, together with suggested approximate timings, is:

What did we do last time?	5–10 minutes
On the agenda: Why are we doing this?	5 minutes
Warm up	5 minutes
Listen to this	10 minutes
Check your grammar	10 minutes
Do it yourself	10 minutes
Sounds good	15 minutes
It's time to talk	20 minutes
Remember → What did we do today?	5 minutes
→ Follow up	

Listen to this

Logistics
Always make sure that you are ready to switch on your cassette or CD in the right place before the lesson starts.

Introducing listening
Introduce each track by saying in broad terms what students are going to hear and why. Make sure students have read the rubrics and that they understand what they have to do.

Listening for gist
The instruction to the teacher in the Teacher's notes is always simply to 'Play track 1.1'. It is for you to decide whether to play the track or part of the track more than once or not. However, playing any track more than three or four times altogether is likely to lead to boredom, so avoid any temptation to do so. Tell students that very often it's best to listen for the main message and not to worry about not understanding every word. In real life, there are rarely more than one or two chances.

Listening tasks
Specific suggestions are made in the Student's Book or the Teacher's notes for individual units, but you can also ask them:
- if they can predict part of a track from what they know about it before they listen
- if they can reproduce parts of a track after they have listened to it
- to listen for examples of particular words or types of word or grammar examples.

Tapescripts
You can encourage students to make use of the tapescripts at the back of the Student's Book for reading at the same time as they listen; and for doing grammar and vocabulary searches of texts they have already heard.

Check your grammar

The syllabus
- The grammar points taught in the type 1 units have been identified as being those of most use to working people. The grammar syllabus is selective rather than comprehensive in order to achieve a good balance between this and the other components of the syllabus –

work-related and general vocabulary, communication skills, and so on.
- For information about particular grammar points and how to handle them in class, we strongly recommend *Grammar for English Language Teachers* by Martin Parrott (Cambridge University Press 2000).

Activating passive knowledge
For any given grammar point, you can ask students some basic questions to check the extent of their knowledge. They may have notions of the point in question and the listening will have jogged their memory. Otherwise, you can vary your approach from lesson to lesson. For example:
- First present the information given in a grammar section, then practise the points by filling the gaps; or
- Ask students to elicit rules from the listening extract they have heard or from the tapescript of the listening, and then do the gap-filling exercise; or
- Ask students to do the gap-filling exercise and then to formulate rules alone or in pairs or as a whole class.

Grammar reference
Always refer them to the Grammar reference section. Make sure students know where it is, and, if appropriate, go through it with them.

Sounds good
Tell students each time that this is the pronunciation part of the lesson. Pronunciation is important but it can also be fun and can appeal to a different kind of learner, some of whom may be less confident about other areas of language. Find out which students have a good ear and the ones who are good mimics, and exploit their talents in presentation and feedback. For example, in Unit 16, encourage them to really accentuate the accented syllables to the point of exaggeration since it is more likely to resemble a native speaker pattern if they do this.

Teaching type 2 units

Unit structure and timing

The structure of type 2 units, together with suggested approximate timings, is:

What did we do last time?	5 minutes
On the agenda: Why are we doing this?	5 minutes
Warm up	5 minutes
Read on	15 minutes
The words you need	10 minutes
It's time to talk	15 minutes
Communicating at work	30 minutes
Remember → What did we do today?	5 minutes
→ Follow up	

Read on
The Read on sections of these units are designed to develop students' ability to skim, scan and read for gist. Although tasks vary from unit to unit, the reading typically asks students to match headings with paragraphs, which involves reading for gist, and then to answer some comprehension questions.

Procedure
A standard procedure for this section is as follows:

1
1. Read the rubric and the four questions or headings. What do they think is the best order before they read the paragraphs?
2. Ask the students to skim the four paragraphs before they do the matching. Give them 20 or 30 seconds (more in the early units and less in the later ones).
3. When they have finished, check their answers and ask them how they proceeded: which key words did they spot in the text which helped them to do the task?

2
1. Read the rubric and the questions.
2. Ask them to read the four paragraphs in more detail and do the exercise.
3. Check their answers.
4. Ask them to do a vocabulary search based on the theme of the text or the main vocabulary area of the unit, or to do a grammar-based search, for example to find adjectives or verbs of a certain kind.

Variations on the above are to:
- read the headings with the students and ask them to suggest sentences that they might find in the texts, before they actually read them
- ask students to cover up the headings, read the paragraphs and then write their own headings – on their own or in pairs
- do the same but this time with you reading the paragraphs aloud to the class or students taking turns to read them to each other.

Reading in other contexts in the Student's Book
More generally, the instruction 'Read' in the Teacher's notes for any unit can be handled in various ways:
- Students can read silently.
- Individual students can take turns reading aloud.
- You can read aloud to them.
- Students can read to each other in pairs.

If there is no specific suggestion, do different things at different times; and ask the students what they want to do.

The words you need
Suggestions are provided in each set of Teacher's notes.

Communicating at work
Suggestions are provided in each set of Teacher's notes.

Teaching type 3 units

Unit structure and timing
The structure of type 3 units, together with suggested approximate timings, is:

What did we do last time?	5–10 minutes
On the agenda: Why are we doing this?	5 minutes
Warm up	5 minutes
Social English dialogues	15 minutes
Have a go	10 minutes
Listen to this	10 minutes
The words you need	10 minutes
It's time to talk	20 minutes
Remember → What did we do today?	5 minutes
→ Follow up	

Social English dialogues
The objective of these dialogues is to equip students with useful survival English with real takeaway value, and, although the format is the same in every type 3 unit, you can handle them in different ways from lesson to lesson. The standard procedure (also given in the Teacher's notes to Unit 3) is as follows:

1. Ask students what they can see in each of the four pictures accompanying the dialogues.
2. Ask students to fill the gaps with words and phrases from the box, working alone or in pairs.
3. Play the appropriate track so that students can listen and check their answers.
4. Check the answers with the group. Do some vocabulary checking questions, if appropriate.
5. Ask the students to read the dialogues in pairs, reversing roles if you have time.
6. Ask selected pairs to perform for the class and give feedback on their performances.

This formula can of course be varied. For example, you can:
- ask students to listen to the appropriate track as they fill the gaps in the dialogues
- cover the box on the page and fill the gaps as they listen
- cover the box and predict the words which will fit the gaps and then check by looking at the box
- cover the box and predict the words which will fit the gaps and then check by listening to the track.

Use the standard procedure in the first one or two units (Units 3 and 6) and then vary the formula thereafter.

Have a go
This section leads straight on from the previous one and provides opportunities for less controlled practice of the social English dialogues. Once again you can adopt a standard procedure as follows:
1. Ask them to cover the dialogues.
2. Get students, working in pairs, to replicate the situation in each of the four dialogues. Stress that they are not expected to remember the exact words of the original dialogues but that they should try to produce appropriate language each time.
3. Ask selected pairs to perform for the class and give feedback on their performances.

The main variation could be to ask students to think of and practise another dialogue relating to the same theme. They can then perform for other students, who have to identify the situation.

The words you need
Suggestions are provided in each set of Teacher's notes.

3 Teacher's notes: Units 1–30

1 Nice to meet you

Starting up the course
Read the section on Starting up the course on page 13 and decide how you want to:
- introduce yourself
- introduce the students to each other
- introduce the material.

On the agenda: Why are we doing this?
Read about Type 1 units on page 12, common elements (page 17) and Teaching type 1 units (page 18).

Explain now or later that this is an example of the first of three types of unit. This type normally looks at grammar and pronunciation although introductions are also an important focus at the start of the course. Type 1 units also practise listening.

Tell students the objectives of this lesson:
- to practise **meeting people** in English and to meet the other members of the group
- to practise the **present simple tense**: the tense we use to ask and answer questions when we meet people
- to do some pronunciation work – on **asking questions**.

Reinforce this by writing the key words on the board or OHP.

Classroom language
Check now or during the lesson – if necessary – that students understand the meanings of:

grammar pronunciation tense present question mistake
positive negative below verb
Verbs:
listen check complete match ask reply stress remember

Warm up
- Ask two pairs of students to read the dialogues aloud (not worrying too much about the pronunciation of the names). Can we say that Susie is American or British? Elicit the fact that the German uses his title (Herr) while the Frenchwoman uses her first name. You may also want to give other students the chance to read the dialogues aloud once you have this information.
- Ask the question about formality (note that we have not used 'How do you do?' which we think is rare and outmoded) and ask how people meet visitors at work. Are there any other formulae? (Note: 'Good afternoon' after midday and 'Good evening' but not 'Goodnight'.)

Answers
Susie – Masahiko: Less formal
Duroc – Wollmann: More formal

- Students can now practise their introductions together by standing up and mingling for a couple of minutes. There is a practical and not just a language reason for doing this: students must learn each other's names. Do a (hopefully) quick memory test and be insistent. Making an effort to learn other people's names exercises the same memory faculties that students will need to remember language. If they have problems, get them to make name cards for themselves and do a test at the start of the next lesson.

Also, remind students when saying their name to people from another country to say it slowly and clearly so that someone who may not recognise it has a chance to register it. Exchanging business cards at this stage can help people to register unfamiliar names because it gives them the chance to see a new name written down.

Listen to this

Say who you are
1
- Look at the pictures of Susie and the inline skates and read the captions. Ask checking questions about her name, her job, etc. Ask if anyone has/likes/uses inline skates. Ask if any of them work on stands at exhibitions. Do they like it? etc. Try to ask mainly yes/no questions so that students can focus on listening and comprehension and don't have to worry too much about producing complicated language to answer.
- Tell students that they are going to listen to Susie meeting a visitor to her stand and that when we meet people, we ask and answer questions to get more information.
- Read the rubric and check they understand.
- Play track 1.1 and then check the answers.

Answers
Name: Olga Novotna
Visitor from: Russia
Company activity: Sportswear
Action: No action

2
- Check understanding of 'brochure'.
- Play track 1.1 again and check the answers.
- Ask if they can remember any of the questions Susie asks. Write their efforts up on the board and get the class to agree on the final form before you comment. Write present simple questions separate from the others.

- Now ask what the tense of these questions is as a lead-in to Check your grammar.

Answers

1 T   2 F   3 T   4 F

Track 1.1 tapescript ▶▶

SUSIE: Good morning.
OLGA: Morning.
SUSIE: Susie Smith, can I help?
OLGA: Hello, Olga Novotna. Nice to meet you. I'm just looking, thanks. It's very interesting.
SUSIE: Thank you. Is this your first visit to Expo?
OLGA: Yes, it is.
SUSIE: Where are you from?
OLGA: Russia.
SUSIE: Russia. Really? Where do you live?
OLGA: In a small town near Moscow.
SUSIE: How far from Moscow?
OLGA: About 20 kilometres. But the company is in Moscow so I get the train in every day.
SUSIE: Right. And who do you work for?
OLGA: For TechnoSport, a sportswear manufacturer.
SUSIE: OK. Would you like one of our brochures?
OLGA: Yes, thanks.
SUSIE: You're welcome. Here. Take two.
OLGA: OK. Nice meeting you. Maybe see you later.
SUSIE: Yes. Nice to meet you. Thank you. Bye.

Check your grammar

The present simple 1

Read the introductory sentence and ask students to complete the gaps alone or in pairs. Check the answers with the class. If necessary, underline the formation of question and negative forms of present simple verbs and the present simple of the verb *to be* by asking for examples of these forms and writing them on the board.

Follow this with some round-the-class drilling for each of the three main points:
- Present simple, e.g. *Where do you live?*
- *To be*, e.g. *Where you from (originally)?*
- *Have/have got*. First of all, show how these can be used interchangeably by asking the same question (which you could write on the board) in two different ways, e.g. *Do you have a car? Yes, I do. / Have you got a car? Yes, I have.* Then drill with other questions, e.g. *Do you have a flat in New York? Have you got a dog?*

Answers

1 do   2 are   3 is   4 am   5 am   6 have   7 do   8 Have

Refer students to the Grammar reference section for this unit on page 110 of the Student's Book and, if appropriate, go through it with them.

Do it yourself

1 Ask students to do this exercise on their own or in pairs, then check the answers. Explain mistakes and check again with supplementary examples of your own.

Answers

1 Do you work for IBM?
2 Do you have (any) children? / Have you got (any) children?
3 I don't work in Paris.
4 We work near Milan.

2 After students have done this in pairs, they can complete the five half-sentences on the left-hand side of the exercise with information about themselves, e.g. I work for Siemens; I come from the south of Spain.

Answers

1 I work for a British company.
2 I come from the north of England originally.
3 I live in Croydon, about 20 kilometres from London.
4 I'm a personal assistant.
5 I go to the US about six times a year on business.

3 After students have done the pairwork exercise, ask selected pairs to perform for the others. You can also ask which is the best order for asking these questions when you meet someone for the first time.

Answers

1 c   2 e   3 d   4 b   5 a

4 Students can do this on their own or in pairs. After they have filled in the gaps, play them track 1.2 so they can check their answers.

Answers

1 are   2 I'm   3 from   4 Do   5 come   6 don't
7 work   8 do   9 make   10 sell

Track 1.2 tapescript ▶▶

SUSIE: So, where are you from, Maria?
MARIA: I'm from Italy.
SUSIE: Really? Are you from Rome?
MARIA: No, I'm not. I'm from Milan. Do you know Milan?
SUSIE: Yes, I went there on holiday last year. It's a lovely place.
MARIA: Yes, it's beautiful. Do you come to Italy often?
SUSIE: No, I don't travel much, maybe two or three times a year for business.
MARIA: Which company do you work for?
SUSIE: I work for Skateline.
MARIA: Skateline? Yes, I know the name. What do you do exactly?
SUSIE: We make inline skates. And you? What do you do?
MARIA: We sell bicycles.

Sounds good

Reply questions

Read the introduction, getting whoever reads to stress the 'you' in the second line strongly.

1 Play track 1.3 and ask students to practise in pairs after listening to the track. Tell students not to be afraid to exaggerate the stress on the repeated 'you': what may sound exaggerated to them may sound fairly normal to a native speaker.
2 Ask students to work in pairs again. Get selected pairs to perform for the rest of the class. Ask for the class's feedback on who has replicated the stress patterns well.

Track 1.3 tapescript ▶▶
See Student's Book.

It's time to talk

Students can practise what they have learnt in this unit and also use the opportunity to get to know each other much better. Organise a non-alcoholic cocktail party (see Serial pairwork in the Introduction on page 16). They should try to get one piece of information about each partner's job, organisation, family and home.

It could be useful to check the Remember section before you start. You may want to use the Extra classroom activity here (see pages 78 and 83).

What did we do today?

Check the Remember section quickly and remind students of the objectives of this lesson.

Follow up

Encourage students to:
1 write sentences about themselves, friends and colleagues in the present simple about:
   - where they come from
   - where they work
   - where they live
   - things they have got, etc.
2 write questions they ask people when they meet for the first time.
3 write down different forms of greeting which they may see or read before the next lesson, for example in the subtitles of films they see on TV or in a graded reader.

2 Helping people to learn

What did we do last time?

Although you may wish to do some review of the work you did in the last lesson, we recommend that you do the main review work in relation to Unit 1 when you come to the next type 1 unit, i.e. Unit 4. This is more challenging for your students since it requires longer recall, but should ultimately provide more continuity and improve learning effectiveness.

On the agenda: Why are we doing this?

Read about Type 2 units on page 12 and Teaching type 2 units on page 18.

Explain that this is an example of the second of three types of unit. This type looks at vocabulary for work and communication skills. The main professional communication skills in business English are presenting, meeting, negotiating, telephoning, writing and socialising. In *English365* Book 1 we focus on writing (emails), telephoning and dealing with visitors. Type 2 units also practise reading.

Tell students the objectives of this lesson (see On the agenda):
- **talking about your job**
- to build vocabulary in the area of **job responsibilities**; check understanding of 'responsibility'
- to practise **getting information by phone**.

Reinforce this by writing the key words on the board or OHP.

Classroom language

Words to check for understanding before or during the unit are:

| noun   preposition   choose   correct (adjective) |
| answer (verb)   vocabulary |

Warm up

We have three people talking about their jobs. Read the three statements and ask students related questions:
- Do you work for a small company?
- Do you like working for a small company / big organisation?
- Do you like writing emails?
- Do you travel in your job? Do you want to travel in your job?

Encourage them to formulate the same or similar questions.

Read on

A new future

Look at the picture of Bonnie and read the caption. Explain now (or later when you come to look at the four paragraphs) that 'Språngbrädan' means 'springboard' in English. Check understanding of 'springboard' by drawing a picture or getting one of your more visual learners to draw a picture on the board or a kinaesthetic learner to mime the action of a diver taking off from a springboard. Can students suggest why the organisation has this name? (Because with a springboard you can go high? You can do beautiful things? It helps you to do more? . . .)

1 Check understanding of words like 'project', 'consultant', 'local' and 'national'. Read the four questions, ask students to look through paragraphs A to D quickly and then do the matching exercise. Give them a minute or so to do this. (As they build their experience, you can ask them to do it more quickly.) If students object that this is not enough time, explain that you want them to develop the habit of looking at a text to get a general idea of its content – just like they must do in their own language. They will have the chance to read the paragraphs in more detail in a moment. Check the answers.

Answers
1 C   2 D   3 B   4 A

2 This time give students time to look at the paragraphs in more detail. Check for comprehension problems as well as checking the answers, and ask students about how difficult the reading was, and why. Getting them to think about the reading process itself and what kind of problems arise will help them in the longer run to improve their reading strategies. You could also get students to ask and answer questions 1–4 in pairs. Then check the answers with the whole class.

> **Answers**
> 1 Helping women to begin in politics and training men and women
> 2 Eastern Europe (for example Moldova and Ukraine)
> 3 Four
> 4 Meeting people

What do you think?

You could write key words relating to good and bad things about people's jobs in two columns on the board.

The words you need ... to talk about your job

1
- Explain that prepositions are important when you talk about your job and your responsibilities.
- Ask students to do the exercise individually or in pairs, then play track 2.1 and check the answers.
- You can also ask them to transfer the same sentences to their own job situation, either working in pairs again or going round the class – selectively if there are a lot of students – and sentence by sentence, e.g.
  STUDENT 1: I'm part of a small consultancy.
  STUDENT 2: I'm part of a big government department.

> **Answers**
> 1 of 2 for 3 in 4 for 5 with 6 of 7 of 8 in

Track 2.1 tapescript ▶▶

See Student's Book.

2 Write on the board:
organise – organiser – organisation – organisational

Explain that many words are part of 'word families' like this one, so when you meet a new word you can quickly get to know several more members of the same group: this is a good way to develop your vocabulary. For example: an *organiser* (person noun) likes to *organise* (verb). S/he is good at *organisation* (common noun) and has good *organisational* skills (adjective). This exercise is about nouns and verbs. Students can do the exercise alone or in pairs. After your answer check, ask students if they can suggest alternative sentences, e.g. for question 5 an alternative would be *I discuss politics a lot in my job*.

> **Answers**
> 1 meet 2 organisation 3 communicate
> 4 manage 5 discussions

3 Ask students to work in pairs. Questions could include:
- Do you work for a big or a small organisation?
- Do you communicate (more) by phone or by email?
- Do you manage a team?

It's time to talk

Students can work with one partner or several (see Serial pairwork in the Introduction on page 16). Get them to stand up and walk around for this if they need recharging; and encourage them to use as much material from Units 1 and 2 as they can. Students should write down answers in the table and report back on their colleagues.

COMMUNICATING AT WORK

Telephoning 1: Getting information

The objective here is to learn and practise some basic telephoning phrases and to learn about the structure of a good phone call. Begin by asking:
- who receives telephone calls in English at work, and how often
- who makes telephone calls in English at work, and how often
- how they feel about phoning in English (easy? difficult? problems?)
- what telephone phrases they know and typically use. You can brainstorm this and write model phrases on the board.

1
- Check understanding of 'training course' and the instructions for the exercise.
- Play track 2.2 and check the answers.

> **Answers**
> Jake Roberts 1   Cancel training ✗
> Call back in ten minutes 1
> Jane Dawson 2   Discuss a problem 1
> No action – talk next week 2
> Julie Simpson ✗   Give help 2
> Send email with information ✗

2 Play track 2.2 again and check the answers. Ask students to read out some of the model phrases and ask which they think they will use and which not. (It's often good to provide alternative expressions so that students can choose which one they feel more comfortable with.) Ask them the question about calls 1 and 2.

> **Answers**
> A Good morning. How can I help you? (1)
>   Who's calling, please? (2)
>   Connecting you now. (1)
>   I'll put you through. (2)
> B It's ... (+ name) (2)
> C Could I speak to ... (+ name)? (2)
>   I'm just calling to ... (+ reason for call) (2)
> D Thanks for calling. (1, 2)
>   Talk to you next week. Bye. (2)
>
> Caller 2 is the better caller. The speaker uses polite greetings and phrases and has a friendly intonation. All these things are missing in the first call.

Track 2.2 tapescript ⏩

Call 1

RECEPTIONIST: CyberProducts. Good morning. How can I help you?
JAKE: Peter Blake.
RECEPTIONIST: Sorry?
JAKE: I want to speak to Peter Blake.
RECEPTIONIST: Connecting you now.
JAKE: OK.
PETER: Peter Blake.
JAKE: Peter. We need a meeting tomorrow to discuss the training course. We have a big problem.
PETER: Sorry, who's calling, please?
JAKE: It's Jake Roberts.
PETER: OK, look Jake, I'm in a meeting right now. Can I call you back in ten minutes?
JAKE: OK.
PETER: Oh ... fine. Thanks for calling.

Call 2

RECEPTIONIST: CyberProducts. Good morning.
JANE: Good morning. Could I speak to Peter Blake, please?
RECEPTIONIST: Certainly. Who's calling, please?
JANE: It's Jane Dawson.
RECEPTIONIST: Just a moment, I'll put you through.
JANE: Thanks.
PETER: Jane. How are you?
JANE: Fine, thanks. And you?
PETER: Fine. How can I help?
JANE: I'm just calling to ask if you want some help with the organisation of the training course next week.
PETER: Thanks, but everything's OK. There's no need for you to do anything.
JANE: Sure?
PETER: Yes, thanks very much.
JANE: OK, great. Have a good training course. Talk to you next week. Bye.
PETER: Yes. Thanks for calling.

3 Look at the plan and emphasise the fact that good structure helps good communication. Then ask students to do the role-play exercise in pairs.

What did we do today?

Check the Remember section quickly and remind them of the objectives of this lesson.

Follow up

Encourage students to:
1 write six or more sentences about their jobs and responsibilities
2 write down phrases for the phone which they use and which they hear other people use.

3 Have a good weekend

What did we do last time?

Although you may wish to do some review of the work you did in the last lesson, we recommend that you do the main review work in relation to Unit 2 when you come to the next type 2 unit, i.e. Unit 5. This is more challenging for the students since it requires longer recall, but should ultimately provide more continuity and improve learning effectiveness.

On the agenda: Why are we doing this?

Read about Type 3 units on page 12 and Teaching type 3 units on page 19.
Explain that this is an example of the third of three types of unit and that this type looks at vocabulary, expression and communication which are useful to working adults in their lives outside work. In every type 3 lesson, students will learn and practise:

- social phrases which are useful for travel or everyday situations
- vocabulary for travel and everyday subjects of discussion and conversation.

Type 3 units will help students manage better when they travel, and when they meet people socially.

Now tell students the objectives of this lesson (see On the agenda):

- to learn some **everyday** phrases useful for **conversation** in (or out of) the office
- to talk about what you do **at the weekends**
- to learn **vocabulary for weekend and free-time activities**.

Reinforce this by writing the key words on the board or OHP. You are also going to develop a list of free-time activities plus collocations on the board during the lesson. Use this for feedback at the end of the lesson and for revision and consolidation later on.

Classroom language

Words to check for understanding before or during the unit are:

| category | cover (verb) | opposite |

Warm up

- Ask students to describe the backdrop photo. Does anyone go sailing? Explain that after some work on social English, you are going to talk about weekend and free-time activities.
- Look at the two Warm-up questions. It could be interesting to compare the answers, especially if students have experience of different countries: offices in some European countries start closing down from lunchtime on Fridays. You can also ask who works at home at the weekend.

It's almost the weekend

- Ask students what they can see in each of the four pictures accompanying the dialogues.
- Ask students to fill the gaps with words and phrases from the box, working alone or in pairs.
- Play track 3.1 so that students can listen and check their answers.
- Check the answers with the group. Ask some vocabulary-checking questions, if appropriate.
- Ask the students to read the dialogues in pairs, reversing roles if you have time.
- Ask selected pairs to perform for the class and give feedback on their performances.

This will be the standard procedure for handling these social English dialogues in type 3 units; see also the Introduction (page 19).

Answers
1 e   2 c   3 b   4 a   5 h   6 g   7 f   8 d

Track 3.1 tapescript ▶▶
Arriving at the office on Friday
A: Hi, John.
B: Morning. How are you?
A: Fine, thanks. And you?
B: Not bad. A bit tired.
A: Never mind. It's almost the weekend.

Going for lunch
A: Ready for some lunch?
B: Yes, good idea.
A: Where do you want to eat?
B: Shall we eat out?
A: Yes, it's Friday. The new Italian place?
B: Great. Let's go.

A weekend away
A: Do you have any plans for the weekend?
B: I'm going to visit my brother.
A: Where does he live?
B: In Stratford-upon-Avon.
A: Stratford? It's a lovely place. Have a good time!
B: Thanks. I will!

Going home
A: I'm going. See you next week.
B: OK, see you.
A: Have a good weekend.
B: Thanks. You too. Bye.

Have a go

Now ask the students to make their own dialogues in pairs using the prompts in the Student's Book:
- Ask them to cover the dialogues on the first page of the unit.
- Get students, working in the same or in different pairs, to replicate the situation in each of the four dialogues. Stress that they are not expected to remember the exact words of the original dialogues but that they should try to produce *appropriate* language each time.
- Ask selected pairs to perform for the class and give feedback on their performances.
- You could also ask them to think of other short dialogues that they can perform in front of the class: asking someone for help with something, asking what someone is planning to do in the evening, talking about a TV programme, etc. Other students can identify the subject of each of the new conversations.

Listen to this

Enjoying your weekend

The second part of the unit aims to build students' vocabulary for talking about free-time activities and things people do at the weekend. Note that Unit 12 deals more specifically with sports and activities involving physical exercise.

1 Look at the pictures and ask students which activity they enjoy most and least.
2 Play track 3.2 and then check the answers.

Answers
SALLY: sailing, walking
HINAWI: sightseeing, swimming
MARTINA: visiting friends, going to the cinema, clubbing, walking, swimming
JOCHEN: astronomy

Track 3.2 tapescript ▶▶
Sally
In the summer I usually like to go sailing on the north Norfolk coast, if the wind is good. We try to go every weekend if possible, but it depends on the weather, obviously. If I don't go sailing then I go walking or maybe stay at home.

Hinawi
Cambridge is so beautiful, you can do lots of things here. There are lots of places you can go sightseeing, for example. But I often go to the swimming pool, I like swimming. Sometimes I go to the local sauna. London is quite close as well and we take the train sometimes.

Martina
I usually work during the weekends, because I need extra money, but if I've got some free time I go out, visit my friends, go to the cinema, clubbing, cycling, walking around Cambridge, swimming.

Jochen
One of my hobbies is astronomy. I've got a telescope and I look at stars and planets and things like that. I usually watch from home but sometimes I put the telescopes in the car and go somewhere where you have a really, really dark sky.

What do you think?

Find out which person, in their opinion, has the most and the least interesting weekend. (If you want to avoid using the superlative form at this stage, you can simply ask: *Do you think that Sally has an interesting weekend? Do you think that Hinawi . . . ?* etc.) Do a class survey and discuss the results.

The words you need ... to talk about your free time

1 Students can do this in pairs. Write up their additional ideas on the board under each heading. Check the answers. Ask students for complete sentences for things they love and hate to do.

Answers
Card and board games: draughts
Reading: non-fiction
Music – listening: classical music
Music – playing: the guitar
Culture: ballet
Couch potato: surfing the net
Food: French
Socialising: going on holiday with friends
Housework: ironing

2 Ask students to match the opposites in pairs and then test each other.

Answers
expensive / cheap   nice / horrible
dangerous / safe   healthy / unhealthy
interesting / boring   fantastic / terrible
fast / slow   good / bad
relaxing / stressful

3 Ask selected students to give you their sentences. Does everyone agree about the sentences they suggest?

It's time to talk

You can organise this as a serial pairwork exercise (see Introduction page 16). As students work on this, walk round helping pairs with vocabulary and taking notes to add to your list of free-time activities on the board. During feedback at the end of the exercise, students can report back on each other. As part of your debriefing, you can try some collocation and vocabulary extension work on selected free-time activities, for example *to play football*, *to go for a walk*, *to work in the garden*, etc. You could also ask each student to provide you with at least one model sentence. Use these to build up a picture of the class's free-time activities as a whole. Ask students additional questions about interesting activities.

What did we do today?
Check the Remember section quickly (by again asking them what they love and hate doing) and remind them of the objectives of the lesson. Look again at the list of free-time activities plus collocations which you have built up on the board during the lesson.

Follow up
Encourage students to write sentences about free-time activities and build up vocabulary lists around one or two selected activities.

4 North and south

What did we do last time?
Do a review of the last type 1 lesson (Unit 1). Remind students of what they worked on (see Teacher's notes for that unit) and do some quick revision as follows. Ask them:
- for the form of the present simple of a common verb like *like* and write it up on the board
- to provide the question and negative forms of another verb, e.g. *read, write*
- the questions: *Where do you live? Where do you work? Who do you work for? What is your job?*
- to make questions with *When*, *Where* and *What* (they can be the same questions).

On the agenda: Why are we doing this?
Tell students the objectives of this lesson:
- to look at the present simple again, this time with '**time words**' like *sometimes* and *never*
- to use the present simple to talk about things you do every day – at work and at home: the **present simple for routines**; check that students understand *routine*
- to do some **pronunciation** work on the third person -*s* (it's up to you whether you want to say more about what this is at this stage).

Reinforce this by writing the key words on the board or OHP.

Warm up
Ask students if they are morning, afternoon, evening or night people. You could ask students to draw a line showing their energy level through a typical day or to describe it with their hand.

Look at the pictures of Anneli and Chiara. Ask checking questions like:
- Where does Anneli/Chiara come from?
- Where's that? (Answer: It's in the north/south of Europe.)
- What are their nationalities? What's your nationality?
- Who does Anneli/Chiara work for?

Listen to this

A working day in the north ... and in the south of Europe
Ask warm-up questions like:
- What time do you get up?
- What time do you usually get to work?
- What do you normally have for lunch?
- Do you sometimes stay late for work?

Ask students to make two or three similar questions to ask you or each other.

Ask them to make sentences about their own working day using *always*, *often*, *usually*, *sometimes* and *never*.

1 Read through the information in exercise 1 about Anneli and Chiara with the students, and explain that they are going to listen to some information about the two women and that they must change any information on the page which is not correct. Then play track 4.1 and check the answers.

> **Answers**
> Anneli: has lunch at 11; usually finishes work at 5
> Chiara: has lunch at 1; has dinner at 8

2 Ask the students to read through the four true/false statements to check understanding. Play track 4.1 again and check the answers.

> **Answers**
> 1 T   2 T   3 F   4 F

Track 4.1 tapescript ▶▶
Anneli
INTERVIEWER: So, what is your job, Anneli?
ANNELI: I'm an assistant administrator with Telia's mobile telephone system.
INTERVIEWER: OK. And how do you organise your working day?
ANNELI: Well, I'm at work at 8, and then first thing, I go through my email. Then we have a short coffee break, have a sandwich, then back to work again.
INTERVIEWER: And when is lunch? I think it's quite early in Scandinavia.
ANNELI: Yeah, for you it's early. I usually eat at 11 for one hour. It's typical in Sweden to bring food to work for lunch. We also have a long coffee break in the afternoon around 2, more drinking coffee, and then go home around 5, something like that.
INTERVIEWER: OK, do you sometimes work late or …?
ANNELI: No, not very often. My boss often works late. With me, maybe I stay until 8 if I have a big project. That can be stressful sometimes …

Chiara
INTERVIEWER: And Chiara, tell me about a typical working day.
CHIARA: OK, I usually get to work at 9. Then I have a cup of tea, very English, I know. I don't have breakfast at home and so I have a little something to eat here in the office. After that, my emails!
INTERVIEWER: Do you prefer working in the morning or the afternoon?
CHIARA: Oh, I'm more of an afternoon person. I'm not very good in the morning.
INTERVIEWER: OK, so what time do you have lunch?
CHIARA: Around 1 o'clock every day. We have a canteen in our company. So maybe we eat for half an hour and go for a little walk just to have some fresh air.
INTERVIEWER: And what time do you usually finish work?
CHIARA: Around 6 o'clock. And that means I have dinner at around 8, more or less. And I go to bed at around 12, not so late.
INTERVIEWER: Right, and do you ever work weekends?
CHIARA: No, never.
INTERVIEWER: And your boss?
CHIARA: She doesn't like to work at the weekend but sometimes, you know, you have a lot to do. But me, no. Weekends are for me, not work!

What do you think?
Ask students which day is more like their own and which day they prefer. Discuss what they find stressful at work.

You could also elicit *east* and *west* and ask students if they know anything about the work routine of someone in a country to the west (for example, for a European student, someone in the US) and to the east (for example, for a European student, someone in Japan or China) and, if so, to describe it, using similar language.

Check your grammar

The present simple 2
Tell students to work through exercises 1 to 3 in pairs or on their own, as appropriate. Then check answers with the whole class. Ask the class several questions with *How often . . . ?* and stress that this is a key question for asking about routines.

Do a quick drill of short answers by asking students questions like:
- Do you work at the weekend?
- Do you work in Milan?
- Does your boss work late every night?

to elicit both positive (*Yes, I do*) and negative (*No, I don't*) responses – ideally with a time expression, e.g. *Yes, I do, sometimes*.

> **Answers**
> **1** 1 does   2 doesn't   3 does   4 is
> **2** always   usually   normally   often   sometimes
>   not very often   rarely   never
> **3** 1 a/every/per   2 every/each   3 times

Do it yourself

1 Give students a few minutes to do exercise 1 on their own and then check answers.

2 Students can do this in pairs. Tell them they need to remember the text because they will have to answer questions about it soon. Ask two or three questions to the whole class about Javier to check general comprehension before students read one sentence each round the class to check answers.

3 and 4 Students may work with the same partner for exercise 3 but should find a different partner for 4. Get students to report back on their questions, write some on the board and use them to question other students.

> **Answers**
> **1** 1 I normally start work at 7.30.
>   2 She travels on business once a year.
>   3 How often does she call you?
>   4 Do you often speak English at work?
> **2** 1 always   2 every   3 usually   4 times   5 a   6 never
> **3** 2 What time does he finish?
>   3 How often does he go to Cuba?
>   4 Where does he go at lunchtime?
>   5 What does he do at the weekend?
> **4** 1 c   2 b   3 e   4 d   5 a

Unit four 27

Sounds good

The present simple third person

- Play track 4.2, then read out the three verbs in the third person – *gets*, *goes* and *watches* – slowly and clearly. Get students in pairs to repeat them to each other several times and check that there is positive criticism of performance.
- Play track 4.3 and check students' answers by asking them first to read out the verb and then to say which type it is. Then ask them to read them all out in pairs.
- Ask students – in pairs or the whole class – to brainstorm more verbs and decide which type they are. Write the results on the board.

Answers		
Type 1	Type 2	Type 3
/s/	/z/	/ɪz/
writes	leaves	relaxes
works	sells	organises
meets	buys	manages
visits	listens	
	does	

Tracks 4.2 and 4.3 tapescripts ▶▶
See Student's Book.

It's time to talk

The subject of this section is stress. Introduce it by reminding students that they heard Anneli say: 'Work can be very stressful sometimes.'

- Ask if they agree and ask them what is stressful in their jobs: short answers, which you can write on the board, are fine.
- With stronger students, show how the word *stress* and its derivations work in English by giving examples like:

I have a lot of stress in my job.	(noun)
My job is very stressful.	(adjective)
I don't normally get very stressed at work.	(adjective)
His work stresses him a lot.	(verb: more usually in US English)

Read the opening text for the Stress Check and then get students to work in pairs on the quiz. Walk around to check on correct question formation and intonation.

When everyone has finished, ask for the results by getting students to report on their partners' answers (paying attention to third person pronunciation). Ask for individual scores and find out who are the most and least stressed members of the class (although don't get too serious: the quiz is intended more as fun than as a piece of scientific enquiry).

Do some final drilling on the question form by saying, for example:
Four cups of coffee
to elicit:
How often do you drink four cups of coffee or more per day?

What did we do today?

Check the Remember section quickly and remind students of the objectives of this lesson.

Follow up

Encourage students to write sentences about themselves, friends and colleagues using the words *always*, *usually*, *normally*, *often*, *sometimes*, *not very often*, *rarely*, *never*.

5 Health care – public or private

What did we do last time?

Do a review of the last type 2 lesson (Unit 2). Remind students of what they worked on (see Teacher's notes for that unit) and do some quick revision as follows.

Job responsibilities
Say the first part of these sentences and ask selected students to complete them:
- I work for . . .
- I work in . . .
- I'm responsible for . . .
- I work closely with . . .
- An important part of my job is . . .

Getting information on the phone
Ask them:
- How do you give your name when you answer the phone? (Possible answers: My name is . . . / This is . . .)
- What else can you say to answer the telephone? (Good morning. Can I help you? / Who's calling? etc.)
- How do you finish the call? (Thanks for calling. / Talk to you tomorrow, etc.)

On the agenda: Why are we doing this?

Tell students the objectives of this lesson:
- to talk about **your organisation** (Notice that we use the word 'organisation' to cover the places where people work in the public sector, as well as private sector businesses.)
- to talk about different kinds of **people you meet in your work**
- to learn how to take **telephone message**s, including work on spelling and numbers.

Reinforce this by writing the key words on the board or OHP.

Classroom language

A word to check for understanding before or during the unit is:

| heading |

Warm up

Get short answers ('I think they're quite good', 'I'm not very happy with the service') to these questions from as many different students as possible rather than long answers from one or two. The questions are to focus the students on the context of the first part of the unit, not to stimulate extended discussion.

Now look at the picture of Margita Westring. (The pronunciation of the name of her hospital may not be obvious to students unfamiliar with Nordic languages! An English rendering might be 'Vecksher'. You might like to spend a couple of minutes discussing strategies for dealing with names that you don't know how to pronounce.)

Ask introductory questions like:
- What jobs do people do in hospitals? (doctor, nurse, consultant, specialist, cleaner, canteen worker . . .)
- Do you know anyone who works in a hospital? Do they like it?

Read on

Working at Växjö Hospital

Before you start, it could be a good idea to check on the Internet or in a newspaper the current value of the Swedish krona against the currency that your students use. At the time of writing: $1 = SKR9.14, £1 = SKR14.3 and €1 = SKR9.16.

Proceed as suggested in the teaching hints for type 2 units in the Introduction (page 18).

> **Answers**
> 1   1 A   2 C   3 B   4 D
> 2   1 2,100
>   2 To focus on the customer.
>   3 250 krona
>   4 She likes to look after people and not only think about profit.

What do you think?

Look at what Margita says about working in the public sector and do a quick classroom survey to find out:
- (if relevant) how many people work in the public and how many in the private sector; and
- how many people agree with her.

Brainstorm and write up on the board the possible reasons for preferring one or the other, for example:

> pay/salary/money   pension   hours   holidays

Remember to keep the vocabulary as simple as possible. Encourage the students to do the same.

The words you need … to talk about people and organisations

1 It's important for students to be able to describe their organisation clearly and accurately so it's worth allowing time for students to make their own sentences after they've done the exercise and then spending time going round the class listening to the sentences they've produced.

> **Answers**
> 1 employees   2 competitor   3 customers   4 supplier
> 5 consultants

2 Ask students to work on their own or in pairs and then check the answers. If they are still unfamiliar with the concept of phrasal verbs, explain that sometimes in English a verb + preposition has a different meaning from the one that its separate parts suggest (compare the literal and phrasal meanings of *look up* – at the ceiling and in the dictionary, as an example) and that phrasal verbs are very common and very important to learn. Then tell students to close their books and do the exercise again. You read out the original sentences but with a pause for the gap (a whistle is handy for this kind of exercise!) and ask them to give you the missing words. Alternatively, you can ask students to do this in pairs, with one in each pair closing the book, then reversing roles.

> **Answers**
> 1 as   2 after   3 for   4 to   5 at   6 with

It's time to talk

Give students a few minutes to prepare a number of sentences about their organisations and the people they deal with inside and outside them. Tell them you are going to ask each of them in turn to make a short (one minute) informal presentation of their organisation to the others and that they can use the sentences they've already written down. Listen to each in turn, asking one supplementary question to each presenter and encouraging other students to ask questions as well. Give language feedback on what you hear. If you make notes clearly on a new piece of paper per student, you can give each of them written feedback as well.

COMMUNICATING AT WORK

Telephoning 2: Taking messages

Before looking at the next section, ask students what they say when they don't understand something in English. Elicit sentences like: *I'm sorry, I don't understand. Could you repeat that, please? Could you speak more slowly, please?* And for difficult names, etc.: *Could you spell that, please?*

Could you spell that, please?

1 Ask students to write down and discuss the abbreviations. Then ask them to read the results back to you so that you can write them on the board. Get the class to agree on the correct version.

2 Ensure that students use the sentences given as they practise with their addresses.

Could I have your number?

- Do a quick check to make sure students can count in English – up to 20 round the class and then selectively up to 100 by writing numbers on the board – and play track 5.1.
- Students should note that in English we pronounce each digit of a telephone number separately – which makes it easier for non-native speakers than in some other

languages! Ask students to work in pairs for exercises 2 and 3 and then do a quick whole class check.
- Ask students if they can spell their own names in English: write their efforts on the board. Then do a check of the English alphabet round the class and explain that learning the alphabet is very important for taking phone messages and for communication on the phone in general.

Track 5.1 tapescript ▶▶

1. 678586
   784367
   488598
   598889
   584989

Can I take a message?

After students have listened to the track and done the conversation practice in pairs, do some quick checking by asking students to complete sentences you begin, for example:
- Can I . . . ?
- Could I . . . ?
- He's not at . . .
- I'm afraid . . .

Answers

1 1 e   2 b   3 f   4 g

Track 5.2 tapescript ▶▶

2
A: Hello.
B: Could I speak to Mr García?
A: I'm afraid he's in a meeting. Can I take a message?
B: Could you ask him to call me back?
A: Of course. Could I have your name and number?
B: Yes, my name's Fiala. That's F-i-a-l-a.
A: Did you say 'F'?
B: Yes, 'F'. Fiala.
A: OK, so that's F-i-a-l-a.
B: Yes. That's right. And my number is 7877545.
A: 787545.
B: No, 7877545.
A: Double 7 – 545. OK, Mr Fiala, I'll make sure he gets the message.
B: Thank you. Goodbye.

What did we do today?

Check the Remember section quickly and remind students of the objectives of this lesson.

Follow up

Encourage students to:
1. learn the alphabet by heart
2. practise counting until they have no problems with basic numbers
3. write sentences about the organisation they work for and the different kinds of people they work with inside and outside the organisation
4. keep a diary (in their own language, if they prefer) of the telephone calls they make and receive in English, how successful they feel each one was and what they could do to improve their performance.

6 Downtown Barcelona

What did we do last time?

Do a review of the last type 3 lesson (Unit 3). Remind students of what they worked on (see Teacher's notes for that unit) and do some quick revision as follows.

Social phrases at the office
Ask students to respond to these phrases with appropriate replies:
- How are you?
- Ready for some lunch?
- Where do you want to eat?
- Do you have any plans for the weekend?
- Have a good weekend.

Ask the same questions to several students to get a variety of replies.

Weekends and free time
Ask students to remind you of what they like doing at the weekend.
Ask for the opposites of words like: *easy, fast, relaxing, expensive, healthy.*

On the agenda: Why are we doing this?

Tell students the objectives of this lesson:
- to learn some key phrases and some useful vocabulary for **shopping**
- to talk about the place **where you live**.

Reinforce this by writing the key words on the board or OHP.

Warm up

- Point out the unit title and ask if *Downtown* is American or British English. Explain or have a student explain that British speakers would talk about the *centre of* Barcelona or the *city centre* or – in some cases – the *business district.*
- Look at the backdrop photo and ask how many students know Barcelona and, briefly, what they think of it. Explain that after practising some useful phrases for shopping, they are going to hear about someone who lives in Barcelona and talk about the places where they live.
- Look at the four statements in the Warm up. Do students share these opinions? Do they love shopping or do they hate it? (This is the lead-in to the social English dialogues.) What do they like shopping for most? Elicit words like *books, food, clothes, wine,* etc. and write words that students may not understand on the board.

Shopping

See the Introduction (page 19): Type 3 units – social English dialogues.

Answers

1 f   2 h   3 i   4 b   5 e   6 a   7 j   8 g   9 c   10 d

Track 6.1 tapescript ⏩

Looking around

A: Hello, can I help you?
B: No, it's OK thanks. I'm just looking.
A: OK. Just ask me if you need some help.

Asking for help

B: Could I try this on, please?
A: Yes, of course. The changing rooms are just there.
B: Thank you.
A: (*A few minutes later*) So, how's that?
B: I'm not sure. It's a bit small. Have you got it in a larger size?
A: No, I'm sorry, we haven't.
B: Oh, I see. I think I'll leave it then.

Asking about the price

B: Excuse me, how much is this, please?
A: It's €47.
B: OK, I'll take it.
A: Fine. You can pay over there.

Asking about payment

A: That's €47, please.
B: Thank you. Can I pay by credit card?
A: Yes, of course. Sign here, please.
B: OK.
A: Here's your card and your receipt is in the bag. Thank you.
B: Thank you. Goodbye.

Have a go

See the Introduction (page 19): Type 3 units. You can also ask students to think of something different to go shopping for and to practise this too so that other students have to guess what it is when they hear the dialogue. They can improvise with regard to size, colour, etc.

After practice in pairs, get them to perform for the whole class.

Listen to this

A shoppers' paradise

Before turning over the page and in preparation for track 6.2, tell students you are now going to practise talking about the place where you live and listen to someone talking about the city where they live: Barcelona. Ask what they think she is going to talk about, encouraging responses specific to Barcelona (like Gaudi's architecture) and also generally applicable ones – good buses, shopping, a beautiful old city, etc.

1 Read the caption by the picture of Montse. Then look at the pictures and identify places students have and have not already mentioned. Explain the listening task, play track 6.2 and then check answers.

> **Answers**
> Gaudi: La Pedrera
> Hand-made gifts
> Fine wines
> Fresh food
> Passeig de Gracia

2 Play track 6.2 again, get students to do this exercise and then check the answers. Ask them how similar the place where they live is to Barcelona; or get them to ask each other the same question in pairs. (If they are from Barcelona, ask them to compare it with Madrid or another city they know.)

> **Answers**
> 1 F   2 F   3 F   4 T

Track 6.2 tapescript ⏩

INTERVIEWER: So, where do you live?
MONTSE: I live in downtown Barcelona, or in the city centre, in Eixample, it's called, which is a cultural area with lots of modernist architecture.
INTERVIEWER: Do you like this area?
MONTSE: Yes, I love it. It's very open, the streets are very wide, the flats and the buildings are not very high … it's a very nice atmosphere.
INTERVIEWER: I think the architecture is nice.
MONTSE: Oh, yes, for example all the Gaudi buildings are around my house. I'm also very near to the Gothic quarter, which is the old centre of Barcelona. It's only ten minutes' walk from my house.
INTERVIEWER: I'm travelling to Barcelona in ten days. Can you recommend something to buy that's typical of the area?
MONTSE: Well, Barcelona is great for shops. I can recommend the hand-made, modernist style gifts. Another thing that is interesting is wine, and Cava.
INTERVIEWER: Is Barcelona good for shopping?
MONTSE: Well, you can find almost anything in Barcelona, it's a shoppers' paradise. But there are two main areas, the Gothic quarter and the Modernist quarter. In the Gothic quarter, you find typical markets where you can buy fresh food, and you have very special shops that are just amazing. In the Modernist area you can find international things – fashion, jewellery, gifts, sophisticated designs. And the prices are good too. It's not so expensive.
INTERVIEWER: Do you have a favourite shop that you like going to?
MONTSE: Let me think … I like all the shops but maybe my favourite area is the Passeig de Gracia, which is a big avenue, and in that area, this is in the Modernist area, I really like all the different shops there. I'm so lucky. I live in a wonderful city, right next to a great shopping area.

What do you think?

Ask students if Montse confirmed, contradicted or added anything to what they had already said about Barcelona. Do they know the city and have any places to recommend? You can get your own ideas from the city's website: www.bcn.es/english/turisme/ivisitar.htm

The words you need ... to talk about where you live

1 Get students to decide in pairs or groups of three which are the correct prepositions, then play track 6.3 for them to check. Students should then make similar sentences to tell each other about where they live before you ask them to tell the whole class.

Unit six 31

> **Answers**
>
> 1 in 2 in 3 near 4 outside 5 on 6 from 7 from 8 in

Track 6.3 tapescript ▶▶|
1 I live in the city centre.
2 I live in quite a small street.
3 I live near the main shopping centre.
4 I live outside Barcelona.
5 Sitges is on the coast.
6 Sitges is about 40 kilometres from Barcelona.
7 Sitges is a small town not far from Barcelona.
8 Barcelona is in the north-east of Spain.

2 Write 'transport' on the board and make sure everyone understands: brainstorm a few standard means of transport as well. Ask them to do this exercise singly or in pairs and then play track 6.4 so they can check their answers. Check that they know how to use each of the transport verbs in the list.

> **Answers**
>
> 1 takes 2 go 3 catch/get 4 walk/get 5 get

Track 6.4 tapescript ▶▶|
SAMANTHA: So, let's plan the weekend. Can we go somewhere?
MONTSE: Yes, what about Sitges? It's a really nice place.
SAMANTHA: How far is it from Barcelona?
MONTSE: Not far. By bus it takes about 40 minutes. Or perhaps we could go by train.
SAMANTHA: I'd like to go by bus. Where do we catch it?
MONTSE: The bus station is quite close – it will only take us about five minutes to walk there.
SAMANTHA: Good! And I've got a friend who lives in Vilanova. Is it far from Sitges?
MONTSE: No, it's quite close. We can probably get there by bus. It's a lovely place.

It's time to talk

This can be fun, especially if students invent a persona for themselves and use this in their role-plays. Make them begin with realistic introductory remarks. (What do people say to each other when striking up a conversation?) Ask selected pairs to perform for the rest of the class.

Remember

If you have time, you could think of a place yourself, e.g. New York, and get students to ask questions using the phrases in the Remember section until they have established its identity.

What did we do today?
Remind students of the objectives of the lesson.

Follow up
Encourage students to:
1 write sentences about the place where they live, using language presented in this unit
2 start a new section in their vocabulary notebook dedicated to words describing the place where they live. They can consult tourist information about the location in brochures and on the Internet. Encourage them to focus on collocation, for example: *take a boat trip*, *go shopping in the local market*, *a historic building*, etc.

7 Changing workspace

What did we do last time?
Do a review of the last type 1 lesson (Unit 4). Remind students of what they worked on (see Teacher's notes for that unit) and do some brief revision work as follows.

Time words
Ask selected students: *How often do you go to the cinema / work at the weekend / speak English at work?*
You can also:
- ask them how many time expressions and adverbs of frequency they can remember
- scramble the adverbs they give you on the board and then ask them to put them in order from most to least frequent.

Routines
Ask: *What time do you start work? / have lunch? / finish work?* etc. Ask students to make similar questions.

Pronunciation of third person -s
- Write up some examples (from Unit 4) on the board and ask students to say them, or
- Write up some examples and ask them to organise them into sound categories, or
- Say the root form of some verbs and ask them to pronounce them with the *-s*.

On the agenda: Why are we doing this?
Tell students the objectives of this lesson:
- **my workplace** – to talk about the place where you work
- **there is/are + nouns** – to use *there is* and *there are* with different kinds of noun (or countable and uncountable nouns, if you know students understand this)
- **pronunciation: linking** – to do some pronunciation work on joining the sounds of words together when we speak. Either now or later, check understanding of 'linking' meaning to put or join things together (draw the links of a chain on the board and/or link two of your fingers together).

Reinforce this by writing the key words on the board or OHP.

Classroom language
Words to check for understanding before or during the unit are:

link, linking (verb)	countable	uncountable	sentence
dialogue	vowel	consonant	arrow

Warm up
Do students have any of the facilities in the pictures? (If necessary, explain that 'facilities' is a word for things you

have in an organisation to make life better or easier – sports facilities, restaurant facilities, facilities for looking after children, etc.) You may want to teach 'table games' while they are looking at the pictures.

Look at the picture of Stein. Ask what they think Telenor is. (Answer: it's the biggest telecoms company in Norway.) Explain that they are going to hear Stein talking about the place where he works.

Listen to this

This is where I work

1 Play track 7.1 and ask selected students for their answers. Find out what the consensus is without commenting as yet.

> **Answers**
>
> Fitness centre
> Table games
> Restaurant

2 Play track 7.1 again and ask selected students for their answers. This time, comment on the answers for both **1** and **2**, replaying the track or referring to the tapescript if appropriate.

> **Answers**
>
> 1 One – the Managing Director
> 2 It's flexible so people can work the hours they want to
> 3 He gets information more quickly because people talk more
> 4 The glass walls – it's not very private and people can see if he is angry

Track 7.1 tapescript ▶▶

INTERVIEWER: So, Stein. Tell me about your great new office.
STEIN: Well, there are 7,000 people here. It's a very big building and the idea is to have all employees in one place. But there are no fixed offices or desks for people. Only one person, the Managing Director, has a personal office. All the other people sit where they can and just plug in their portable computer.
INTERVIEWER: What about paper?
STEIN: There's no paper, or very, very little. We want a paperless office with information on a database.
INTERVIEWER: Do employees like this new office system?
STEIN: Oh, yes. I think it's very, very flexible. People can now work when it's good for them to work.
INTERVIEWER: And in this building, are there a lot of things for staff, like a fitness centre or anything they can do after work?
STEIN: Yes, there's a big fitness centre, which people also like a lot. There are also a lot of table games, and a very good restaurant, which is open after people normally go home. The office has everything you want.
INTERVIEWER: Do you like it?
STEIN: Well, yes, I like it a lot. The important thing for me is that I get information very quickly. In the open office, I hear things which I can use in my work. That's good. People talk more, I think.
INTERVIEWER: Is there anything about it that you don't like?
STEIN: OK, maybe there's one little thing I don't like. Sometimes you know, people are people, and sometimes people don't want to be with people, they want to be alone, if they have a bad day, or if they want to think about something. And the problem for me is that with the glass, all the walls in the rooms have glass walls, people can see me if I get angry, which is sometimes not so good.

What do you think?

Ask the question and do a class survey of the answers.

Check your grammar

Countable and uncountable nouns with *There is ...* / *There are ...*

Explain that in English there are nouns you can count (called 'countable' or 'count' nouns) and nouns that you can't count (called 'uncountables' or 'non-count' nouns). Ask students to find in the tapescripts at the back of their books:
- two or three examples of countables – there are lots so this should be easy
- two or three uncountables – 'paper', 'information' and 'glass' may be more difficult to find. Contrast 'paper' with 'a piece of paper'.

Look at the table in the Student's Book and point out how countables have a singular and plural form; and how we use 'some' with the countable plural and uncountable forms.

Ask the students to fill the gaps in the table. Then check their answers. Can they explain *why* they have written these answers? Then read the notes.

> **Answers**
>
> 1 are   2 some   3 any   4 Are   5 Is   6 aren't

Do it yourself

Ask them to do exercises 1 to 3 alone or in pairs, then check the answers. Use particular sentences to transfer to students' own workplaces, e.g. *Is there a car park for employees in your workplace? Is there a railway station nearby?* etc.

Play track 7.2 to check answers to exercise **2**.

> **Answers**
>
> 1 1 There are two training rooms on the first floor. / There is a training room on the first floor.
>   2 There aren't any private offices on the top floor. / There isn't a private office on the top floor.
>   3 Is there any computer equipment on the first floor? / Is there computer equipment on the first floor?
>   4 There aren't a lot of spaces in the car park. / There isn't a lot of space in the car park.
> 2 1 is there   2 there's   3 there's   4 Is there   5 there are
>   6 Is there   7 there isn't   8 there are   9 Is there
>   10 there are
> 3 1 some / a lot of   2 some / no   3 any / a lot of   4 any
>   5 a lot of / no

Track 7.2 tapescript ▶▶

DAVID: So, is there a car park for employees?
BOB: Yes, there's some space but only for top management.
DAVID: What do other people do?
BOB: Well, there's a railway station nearby so lots of people come by train.
DAVID: I see. What about lunch? Is there a staff restaurant?
BOB: No, but there are a lot of bars and restaurants in the same street.
DAVID: Is there a gym or swimming pool?
BOB: No, there isn't anything like that. But there are two parks across the street and a swimming pool half a kilometre away.
DAVID: Is there somewhere I can get a drink?
BOB: Yes, there are a lot of drinks machines in the building. Let's get something.

4 Before doing this, elicit a sample question about something positive and something negative, e.g.
- Is there a restaurant?
- Is there any space for new people?
- Are there a lot of offices? parking spaces?

And for certain facilities:
- Is that positive or negative?

You could also scramble these words and write them on the board:

travel	trip	money	dollar	training	training course
work	job	trouble	problem		

and ask students:
- to identify the pairs
- to say which is countable and which is uncountable in each pair
- to suggest a sentence for each word.

Sounds good

Linking

Practising linking can not only help students with their pronunciation but can also help them to understand more through better listening. It can also be fun trying to replicate sounds which are perhaps unfamiliar to them.

Start with a quick alphabet check. (Students can also work on this on their own using the Personal Study Book with Audio CD.)

Play tracks 7.3 and 7.4 and ask students to practise saying the examples to each other in pairs and to the whole class. Give other examples to practise and ask students to provide them too.

Answers

1   3 sounds more natural.
2   1 Telenor is a big company.
    2 It's a very big building.
    3 I think it's very, very flexible.
    4 There's a big fitness centre, which is very good.
    5 Yes, I like it a lot.

Track 7.3 tapescript ▶▶

1 There is a big problem.
2 There is a big fitness centre.
3 There are a lot of small cafés.

Track 7.4 tapescript ▶▶

See Answers above.

It's time to talk

Read the instructions and make sure students understand the situation. Nominate pairs and be clear about which student takes which file card.

During the debriefing, find out which solution was preferred and why. This may lead to more general discussion.

What did we do today?

Check the Remember section quickly and remind students of the objectives of this lesson.

Follow up

Encourage students to write six to ten sentences about their own and other places of work using *There is* and *There are*.

8 The A team

What did we do last time?

Do a review of the last type 2 lesson (Unit 5). Remind students of what they worked on (see Teacher's notes for that unit) and do some quick revision as follows.

Your organisation
Ask students to make sentences about their organisation using these words:
- employees
- customers
- competitors (for business organisations)
- suppliers

Taking phone messages
Ask students to give you useful phrases for taking messages. If necessary, give them cues to complete, like:
- I'm afraid he's . . .
- Could I . . . ?
- I'll make sure . . .

On the agenda: Why are we doing this?

Tell students the objectives of this lesson:
- **describing people you work with**
- **meeting visitors.**

Reinforce this by writing the key words on the board or OHP.

Classroom language

Words to check for understanding before or during the unit are:

continue	describe	description	dictionary

Warm up
Read the sentences and ask students to describe themselves. Then look at the picture of Shirley and read the caption.

Read on
We're a great team
1 Give the students half a minute or so – or longer if appropriate – to do the matching exercise, then check their answers. Tell them that you want them to look for the main ideas at this stage, not to read every word.

Answers
1 B   2 E   3 D   4 C   5 A

2 Read the paragraphs again and ask students to do this exercise, then check the answers. This time ask some basic comprehension questions to check and/or also some more general questions like: *What's Jack like? What kind of person is Jean?* You can also ask: *Do you agree with Shirley that sometimes you have to say no to clients?*

Answers
1 John (C)   2 David (D)   3 Katie (E)   4 Jean (B)   5 Jack (A)

What do you think?
Students should quickly identify the two colleagues they think of. You can also ask them if any of Shirley's colleagues are like any of their own.

The words you need ... to describe people
1 At the transfer stage, encourage them to use other words as well to describe their boss, teacher, etc. and write the words they use on the board. They can also categorise these as positive, negative or neutral.

Answers
2 creative   3 impatient   4 competitive   5 direct
6 punctual   7 confident

2 It's important for students to practise and master the expressions: *I'm good at ... / I'm good at doing ...* Ask students to exchange sentences about themselves and colleagues in pairs and then build up their ideas on the board.

It's time to talk
If all the students in the class work in the same organisation, this could be played as a team game with two sides scoring points for correct identifications, either according to the rules of Twenty Questions or with each team starting with ten points and losing a point for every sentence given to them by the other side before they guess correctly.

You may want to use the Extra classroom activity here (see pages 79 and 90).

COMMUNICATING AT WORK
Meeting a visitor at the airport

- Start by asking how many students have to meet visitors in and outside the office. Explain that this part deals with writing about travel details and meeting someone at the airport. If your students don't do it already, they may start doing so once they have practised doing it in class!
- In advance of the input in the Student's Book, you could also brainstorm some phrases they might use in writing an email containing travel details, and phrases you might say to someone you are meeting at the airport (a) who you know, and (b) who you don't know.

Answers
1 1 arrival   2 flight   3 confirm   4 meet   5 take   6 plan
   7 seeing   8 wishes
2 It's good to see you again. How are you?
   Did you have a good trip?
   Can I help you with your luggage?
   The car's in the car park.
   How's the weather back home?

Track 8.1 tapescript ▶▶
SHIRLEY: Hi, Koji. It's good to see you again. How are you?
KOJI: Hello! I'm fine, thanks. What about you?
SHIRLEY: Not too bad. A little tired. Too much work, you know.
KOJI: I know the problem.
SHIRLEY: Did you have a good trip?
KOJI: Not too bad. A little delay when I left but nothing serious.
SHIRLEY: Good. Here, can I help you with your luggage?
KOJI: Thank you. Could you take this?
SHIRLEY: Of course. No problem. Now follow me. The car's in the car park.
KOJI: OK. Wow, it's so warm here. It's beautiful.
SHIRLEY: Yeah, it's been great recently. How's the weather back home?
KOJI: Really cold right now. So this is nice!
SHIRLEY: Good. Well, welcome to the sun! This is it. Let me put your bags in the back and we can …

3 Look at the flow chart. Discuss the ideas with students. Are there other things you can do? Now ask them to role-play dialogues in pairs using the framework in the book and then reverse roles.

What did we do today?
Check the Remember section quickly and remind students of the objectives of this lesson.

Follow up
Encourage students to:
1 write sentences about people they know, both personally and professionally
2 make notes from real life or TV and films of phrases they hear being used when welcoming visitors to a city or country.

Unit eight 35

9 I love Chicago

What did we do last time?
Do a review of the last type 3 lesson (Unit 6). Remind students of what they worked on (see Teacher's notes for that unit) and do some quick revision as follows.

Shopping
Ask students to give you some useful phrases for shopping. If necessary, give them some cues like:
- help
- price
- size
- payment.

The place where I live and work
Similarly, give them cues to make complete sentences about the places where they live, for example:
city centre   countryside   near   shopping centre   outside   north/west/east/south etc.

On the agenda: Why are we doing this?
Tell students the objectives of this lesson:
- to practise language for **getting around a new city** by public transport and taxi; explain that *getting* here means *moving/going/travelling* and elicit or provide *cab* as the American English equivalent of *taxi*
- to talk about **city life** – facilities (see also Unit 7), quality of life and lifestyle.

Reinforce this by writing the key words on the board or OHP.

Warm up
- Look at the backdrop photo. Does anyone know Chicago? Can anyone name some important sights and other places? How can you get around this (or any other big) city?
- Get quick answers to the three questions and note them down or write them on the board: you can use the information later.

Getting around

See the Introduction (page 19): Type 3 units – social English dialogues. When students look at the four pictures accompanying the dialogues, ask if they can name any other possible forms of transport.

> **Answers**
> 1 e   2 b   3 g   4 f   5 h   6 d   7 c   8 a

Track 9.1 tapescript ▶▶
Buying a ticket
A: Hi. Three tickets for the Wendella Lake tour, please. Two adults and one child.
B: That's $22.50, please.
A: Thanks. What time does the next ferry leave, please?
B: At 3 o'clock, in 25 minutes.
A: OK. Thanks.

Taking the train
A: Excuse me. Does this go to O'Hare Airport?
B: No. You need to take the blue line.
A: OK, so where do I go?
B: Go to Lake Street and transfer to the blue line and then take it to the end of the line.
A: Great. Thanks for your help.

Catching a bus
A: Excuse me. Can I get a bus to the Magnificent Mile from here?
B: Yes, you want a number 151 or a 147. Or you can take a cab or walk.
A: When's the next bus?
B: Ten minutes. But they're not always on time.
A: Thanks.

Getting a cab
A: How much is that?
B: That's $10.20.
A: Here you are, $12.00. Keep the change.
B: Thank you.
A: Could I have a receipt?
B: Sure. Here you go. Have a good day.

Have a go

See the Introduction (page 19) : Type 3 units. You can also ask them to think of a different kind of travel situation within a city so that the others have to guess what it is when they hear the dialogue. They can improvise with regard to the place, the kind of journey, etc.

Listen to this
It's my kind of town

Introduce the class to Ellen by looking at her photo and reading the caption.

> **Answers**
> 1 A Lebanese restaurant
>   The Sears Tower
>   Louis Armstrong
>   The Chicago Cubs
>   The Taste of Chicago
>   Al Capone

2 After checking the answers, ask students what they would like to do or see in Chicago based on the sentence beginning: *I'd like to . . .*

> **Answers**
> 1 T   2 F   3 F   4 T

Track 9.2 tapescript ▶▶
INTERVIEWER: So, where do you live, in Chicago or just outside?
ELLEN: I live in the centre of the city in an area called the Magnificent Mile, or the Gold Coast, which is the centre of all restaurants, bars and shopping.
INTERVIEWER: And do you like living in Chicago?
ELLEN: Like it? I love it. It's beautiful, really beautiful. It's a nice place to live, very clean and organised. Maybe the thing I like most about it is the number of ethnic restaurants. I think you can eat food from any country in the world here.

INTERVIEWER: What's your favourite restaurant then?
ELLEN: My new thing is Middle Eastern so I go to Persian, Turkish and Iraqi restaurants, or my favourite, yes, of course, is a fantastic Lebanese restaurant – Lebanese food is my favourite – where for five bucks you get an amazing meal and the best lentil soup in the world!
INTERVIEWER: What is there to see and do?
ELLEN: Well, we are famous for the first skyscraper in the country. I think it went up in 1885. And we have the Sears Tower, the tallest building in North America, OK not the world, but tourists typically do that.
INTERVIEWER: Chicago is famous for music too?
ELLEN: Sure, Chicago *is* music. Louis Armstrong was big here and you can listen to lots of blues and jazz. But we have a lot of things here like a jazz festival, a film festival, and a baseball team, the Chicago Cubs – and do you know the Taste of Chicago?
INTERVIEWER: No, what's that?
ELLEN: It's a big eating day – like a very big barbecue in the park. Three million people come and visit for the day in summer and eat, eat, eat – 237,000 pieces of pizza and 120,000 turkey legs. It's really amazing and the quality is excellent. You know, fast food is part of the culture. The first McDonald's was in 1955 in Chicago.
INTERVIEWER: Is there anything you don't like? People have this idea that it's quite dangerous, is that true?
ELLEN: Well, it's famous for Al Capone, of course. But I know New York City and I can say I feel safe here in Chicago. No, I can maybe say it's expensive but that's all. I don't want to live anywhere else. Chicago is my home and it's great!

What do you think?

If not Chicago, another US city or elsewhere? There is ample opportunity to expand on this, so decide whether you want to ask them about favourite cities here or later on (if you have not already exploited this in Unit 6): see also the next section.

The words you need ... to talk about city life

1 Students can do this in pairs. If they live in the same place, they can talk about this first and then about different cities if they come from different places originally or know another city well.

Answers
1 c   2 j   3 h   4 g   5 a   6 i   7 b   8 d   9 f   10 e

2 Encourage students to think of other words to describe where they live.

Answers
1 busy / quiet
2 safe / dangerous
3 clean / dirty
4 noisy / quiet
5 high / low
6 warm / cool
7 awful / excellent
8 beautiful / ugly
9 full / empty

It's time to talk

Ask students to work in pairs and to reverse roles before getting selected pairs to perform for the class.

Remember
You could expand on the notes in the book by saying one of the adjectives from the unit and getting students to respond with the name of a city they know, e.g.
Quiet → Bonn
Clean → Zurich, etc.

What did we do today?
Remind students of the objectives of the lesson.

Follow up
Encourage students to:
1 write sentences describing a city they know – what one can do and see and what kind of place it is
2 find a simple text in English about a city in a brochure or on the Internet and to add useful vocabulary from this to the Places section of their vocabulary notebook.

10 Eating around the world

What did we do last time?
Do a review of the last type 1 lesson (Unit 7). Remind students of what they worked on and do some brief revision work as follows:

Workplace / countables and uncountables
- Ask students to tell you about the facilities in their workplace using *There is* and *There are*.
- Give students sample nouns and ask them if they are countable or uncountable, e.g. *money, space, time, office, cup of coffee, water, chair, information*, etc.

Linking words
Ask students to repeat some sample sentences, like:
- It's an interesting place.
- I like it a lot.
- There's a pool in the basement.
- It's a lot of money.

Emphasise the rhythm as well as the aspect of linking as they say them.

On the agenda: Why are we doing this?
Tell students the objectives of this lesson:
- to talk about different kinds of **food**
- **comparing** things (check understanding of 'compare')
- **pronunciation** – to practise pronouncing **comparative forms**.

Reinforce this by writing the key words on the board or OHP.

Unit ten 37

Classroom language

Words to check for understanding before or during the unit are:

| compare | comparison | comparative | schwa | syllable |
| superlative | weak | strong | underline | |

Warm up

- Ask the students to do the matching exercise and check the answers. The question that follows can be about the five foods shown or about different national cuisines. You can ask either or both.
- Ask if food is important in their working lives as well as in their private lives.
- Look at the picture of Ablaziz and read the caption. Explain that they are going to hear Ablaziz comparing food in different countries.

Answers

Morocco: couscous
India: curry
England: roast beef and Yorkshire pudding
Mexico: burritos
France: foie gras

Listen to this

Favourite food

Answers

1 England, France, India
2 1 T   2 T   3 F   4 T

Track 10.1 tapescript ▶▶

INTERVIEWER: Ablaziz, you're from France. Can I ask you first, what do you think about English food?
ABLAZIZ: Well, English food for me can be very, very good, perhaps a little heavy but very good. I think the idea of bad English food is a cliché now. The food is better than in the past.
INTERVIEWER: But you think English food is heavier than French food?
ABLAZIZ: Yes, it is heavier than French food. French food is lighter. In England I think you often have a big piece of something like meat, and often fatty food, which is maybe too heavy.
INTERVIEWER: What about price? Is English food more expensive?
ABLAZIZ: I think, generally, the price is similar. But in London, it's interesting, it's more expensive than you find in Paris, much more expensive.
INTERVIEWER: Which food do you like the most?
ABLAZIZ: Italian food, because it's very simple. There's a lot of pasta, a lot of starters with vegetables, a lot of sauces so I think it's quite light, not heavy. But I have to say, if I have a birthday, I eat foie gras, a typical French dish.
INTERVIEWER: I know you travel to the Middle East sometimes. How is the food there?
ABLAZIZ: In Jordan and in Israel, it's like Mediterranean food, like Greek food, very light with lots of small dishes and different choices. Nice.
INTERVIEWER: Do you think the food there is better than in Europe?
ABLAZIZ: No, I can't say that it's better. It's different. French food and Italian food is the food I prefer but I can't say which is the best.
INTERVIEWER: Do you like spicy food?
ABLAZIZ: Yes, Indian, for example. Indian is spicier than French food generally. And yes, I like it.
INTERVIEWER: Finally, just a question about food and business. People say that eating is an important part of business. Do you agree?
ABLAZIZ: Yes, you meet a lot of people in business around lunch or dinner. Restaurants are the best place to discuss business, with good food and a good atmosphere. So it's good because, for me, eating good food is one of the most important things in life.

What do you think?

How important is food to your students (e.g. on a scale of 1 to 5)? Is it more important than sleeping? than work? than sport?

Point out that the four true/false sentences contain three comparatives and one superlative. Can they identify the superlative? What is it the superlative of? Can they formulate any rules for sentences like:
- Jean is older than Céline.
- Helmut is taller than Sven.
- This offer is more interesting than that one.

before looking at the next section?

Check your grammar

Comparative and superlative adjectives

Look at the table with the students before asking them to do the exercise. Check understanding of *most/least*, etc. and point out basic features like *than* and *the* with the superlative.

Check the answers and support the information in the table with teacher- and student-generated sentences about people in the class using the comparative and superlative forms of adjectives like *big, small, rich, poor, interesting, boring, tall, short,* etc.

Answers

1 cheaper   2 tastier   3 tastiest   4 most   5 more   6 least
7 best   8 bad

Do it yourself

- Students can work through all three exercises in pairs or do the first two alone and then go into pairs to test each other.
- Play track 10.2 for students to check the answers to exercise 2.
- Encourage them in exercises 2 and 3 to come up with their own examples as well as those suggested in the book and write up as many of the adjectives that you hear on the board as you can.

> **Answers**
>
> **1**
> 1 I learn vocabulary faster than I learn grammar.
> 2 For me, English grammar is easier than French grammar.
> 3 My Spanish is worse than my French.
> 4 The most important language for international business is English.
>
> **2**
> 1 Fresh fruit is healthier than chocolate.
> 2 Salmon is cheaper than Russian caviar.
> 3 Champagne is more expensive than Cava.
> 4 A sandwich is quicker to eat than a meal in a restaurant.
> 5 Indian food is spicier than English food.
>
> **3**
> 1 The Knightsbridge is **more** expensive than Chez Pierre.
> 2 Gianni's is the **biggest** restaurant in the guide.
> 3 The Mogul is **smaller** than Gianni's.
> 4 Chez Pierre is the **least** expensive / **cheapest** restaurant in the guide.
> 5 The Knightsbridge has the **best** food in the guide.

Track 10.2 tapescript ▶▶|
2
1 Fresh fruit is healthier than chocolate.
2 Salmon is cheaper than Russian caviar.
3 Champagne is more expensive than Cava.
4 A sandwich is quicker to eat than a meal in a restaurant.
5 Indian food is spicier than English food.

Sounds good

Weak stress 1

Tell students that you are going to focus on how to say the comparative forms they have been practising. Play the two sentences on track 10.3 and ask students:
- what they notice
- to repeat as accurately as possible.

Then read the rubric and check understanding of the key concepts: weak and strong stress and the schwa. Explain that the schwa is the commonest vowel sound in English and write the phonetic symbol on the board. If they have dictionaries, ask them to find more examples of the schwa.

Track 10.3 tapescript ▶▶|
See Student's Book.

2 Work through the exercise by playing track 10.4. Give students lots of opportunities to practise (and also to work on comparatives again!).

> **Answers**
> 1 We're _politer than the_ rest.
> 2 We're _faster than the_ rest.
> 3 We're less expensive _than the_ rest.
> 4 We're _the_ biggest in _the_ world.
> 5 We're _the_ best in _the_ world.

Track 10.4 tapescript ▶▶|
See Student's Book.

It's time to talk

The subject of this section is comparing hotels for a weekend break. Check the rubric and then organise the students into pairs or groups of three. Find out from the debriefing which hotels were finally chosen and why.

What did we do today?
Check the Remember section quickly and remind students of the objectives of this lesson.

Follow up
Encourage students to write sentences comparing different aspects of their work, food, or another subject. Consumer catalogues are a good source of comparative information on which to base a simple report.

11 Nice work

What did we do last time?
Do a review of the last type 2 lesson (Unit 8). Remind students of what they worked on (see Teacher's notes for that unit) and do some quick revision as follows.

Describing people
How many words can students remember from Unit 8 for describing people?
Ask them to make two or three sentences about one or more of the following:
- a colleague
- a customer
- a neighbour or other.

Meeting visitors
Ask students to recall the stages in the meeting at the airport which they practised.
Ask selected students to perform a brief role-play of such a meeting for the others.
Ask the class to provide you with key phrases for this kind of meeting.

On the agenda: Why are we doing this?
Tell students the objectives of this lesson:
- to talk about **what you want from your job**
- to build **vocabulary to talk about work**
- to practise **writing emails**.

Reinforce this by writing the key words on the board or OHP.

Classroom language
A word to check for understanding before or during the unit is:

| expression |

Unit eleven 39

Warm up

1 Look at the cartoons. Students can formulate simple sentences like:
   - I like the money but I don't like the stress.
   - I like my colleagues but I don't like the travel.
2 Look at the picture of Paul and read the caption.

Read on

Homeworking

1 Pre-reading: read the headings with the students and ask them to suggest sentences that they may find in the text, before they actually read it.

Answers
1 D   2 B   3 A   4 C

2 Give students a chance to read the paragraphs more carefully before they answer the questions. As you check the answers, do a brief transfer by asking questions like:
   - Do you ever work from home?
   - What do you do to relax?

Answers
1 Gardening; playing football with friends; sitting in the garden
2 He prefers to work alone; can go directly to his desk with no traffic problems; liked to look after the children when they were younger; likes working with his wife
3 His Internet connection
4 He loves working in education and with writing

What do you think?

What are the advantages and disadvantages of working at home? (You can tell the true story of the homeworker who puts on his office clothes every weekday, goes out of the house and round the block before coming back and sitting down to another day at the computer.)

The words you need ... to talk about work

This vocabulary will help students talk about their work in general terms.

1 After the exercise, ask students if they can make their own sentences using the verb 'work'. You could also test them by giving them words from the box and asking them to give you complete sentences.

Answers
1 from / at   2 at   3 in   4 abroad   5 alone   6 part-time

2 Ask students to reformulate the sentences which don't describe them, e.g.
   - I have a small office.
   - I don't travel a lot in my job.

Answers
1 d   2 g   3 a   4 f   5 h   6 b   7 c   8 e

It's time to talk

Treat this as a serial pairwork activity. Allow a little time for students to formulate their questions before starting.

COMMUNICATING AT WORK

Emails 1: Giving your emails a clear structure

Ask students if they understand the importance of KISS – Keep It Short and Simple, or, more bluntly, Keep It Simple, Stupid – the golden rule for writing in English and one which will make their lives much easier.

1 Exercise 1 exemplifies this. After the exercise, ask students to provide you with other appropriate expressions for each of the four stages to build more short, simple emails. This should boost their confidence about writing in English.

Answers
1 1 c   2 d   3 b   4 a
2 1 b   2 d   3 c   4 a
3 1 Dear Simon
     We are having a meeting with Jayne Keegan in Berlin on 21st January.
     Can you meet her at the hotel and drive her over?
     Thanks.
     (Name)
   2 Dear Christine
     We need to finalise a price for the XZ34.
     Could you call me tomorrow?
     Regards
     (Name)
   3 Dear Karl
     There is a production problem in Oslo.
     Could you give Henrik a ring on 0047 9843 768767?
     Best wishes
     (Name)

Note key phrases and good structure as much as possible during your feedback.

What did we do today?

Check the Remember section quickly and remind students of the objectives of this lesson.

Follow up

Encourage students to:
1 write sentences about their attitudes towards their work
2 keep a record of any emails they write before the next lesson, asking them to think about the structure of each one.

12 Do you salsa?

What did we do last time?
Do a review of the last type 3 lesson (Unit 9). Remind students of what they worked on (see Teacher's notes for that unit) and do some quick revision as follows.

Getting around
Ask them for useful phrases for:
- buying a ticket for a bus or train
- asking for directions in the subway
- asking how to get from A to B
- paying a taxi driver.

You could also ask students to do quick mini-dialogues based on these situations. If they all come from the same place, you can ask them to imagine they are tourists in the place where they live. If they are not, they can base their instant dialogues on a famous city that all or most of them know.

City life / where you live
Ask students which their favourite cities are and why. They should name three things in general and three particular places they like, for example, for London:
- general: the museums, the parks, the shops
- particular places: Tate Modern, Regent's Park, Harrod's.

On the agenda: Why are we doing this?
Tell students the objectives of this lesson:
- to learn phrases for **responding** (replying, reacting) to different kinds of **news**
- to learn vocabulary for talking about **sport and physical exercise**.

Reinforce this by writing the key words on the board or OHP.

Warm up
- Ask what is happening in the backdrop photo of the salsa dancers and whether anyone has any experience of salsa or other kinds of dancing. Explain that you are going to talk about free-time activities involving physical exercise after you have worked on the social English dialogues on the first page of the unit.
- Ask students the first two Warm-up questions.
- Do a quick class survey to find out who prefers taking some kind of exercise and who prefers to watch sport (or do neither). Can you divide them into team players and individualists as well?
- Ask if anyone has a job involving physical exercise. If so, what kind of exercise? Students could mime actions if they don't have the vocabulary for this.

I've got news for you

Ask students first of all to look at the four pictures accompanying the dialogues and give their own examples of some good news, interesting news, bad news and surprising news.

> **Answers**
> 1 g   2 d   3 c   4 h   5 b   6 f   7 a   8 e

Track 12.1 tapescript ▶▶
Responding to good news
A: Hi. Good weekend?
B: Yes, very. I have some news. My wife's pregnant.
A: Wonderful. Congratulations!
B: Thanks. We're very happy.
A: Oh, good. We must celebrate.

Responding to interesting news
A: Hey, Peter. I've got an email from China.
B: Really?
A: Yes, it's a new customer, I think. They want information about our products.
B: Great. Please tell me if you hear any more from them.
A: Of course I will.

Responding to bad news
A: So you leave for the US tonight?
B: Don't ask! My trip's cancelled!
A: Why's that?
B: Because I have to stay here for a meeting with my boss.
A: Oh, well, never mind. Now you can come to Helen's party tonight.

Responding to surprising news
A: See you tomorrow.
B: Yeah, see you. What are you doing tonight?
A: I'm not sure yet. I might go jogging.
B: You're joking! I don't believe it. You hate sport.
A: Yes, but I need the exercise.

Have a go

You can ask them to think of other short dialogues that they can perform in front of the class (perhaps based on examples of different kinds of news they gave you before you started work on the dialogues): other students can decide whether the news is good, bad, interesting or surprising.

Listen to this

I hate watching TV

1 The second part of the unit aims to build students' vocabulary for talking about sporting activities and activities involving physical exercise. ('Roisin' is pronounced 'Ro-shin'.)

> **Answers**
> 1 Ben: tennis, squash, motorcycle racing
>   Alison: flying, scuba diving
>   Roisin: salsa dancing, swimming
> 2 Ben: Winning is not important. I like to socialise.
>   Alison: It's good exercise. I like being alone.
>   Roisin: I have to relax after work. I hate sport on TV.

Track 12.2 tapescript ▶▶
Ben
INTERVIEWER: So Ben, do you do any sport?
BEN: At the weekend, I do a lot of sport. I play tennis and squash, the usual things. But I also do a lot of motorcycle racing – I have a 1954 Triumph 650 cc. I usually race with around 20 other bikes at about eight to ten meetings a year. It's a lot of

work to maintain the bike but it's very exciting. I never win, but that's not important. I just like to meet people who have the same interest.

Alison

INTERVIEWER: And Alison, are you a sporty person?

ALISON: Yes, I am. I like flying and I also sometimes go scuba diving. For the flying, I go around six times a year – and for scuba diving, maybe around eight times. The only problem is that both sports are quite expensive. Flying costs about £100 per hour and scuba diving about the same. And another thing with scuba diving, the sea around the UK is really cold!

INTERVIEWER: Do you like the danger of these sports?

ALISON: Flying and scuba diving are not dangerous. No, I like flying because I like being alone in the air and so I can relax. And diving, I like it because it's good exercise.

Roisin

INTERVIEWER: Roisin, how about you? Do you do much sport?

ROISIN: Not really sport. I go dancing, salsa dancing, once a week – anything from two to four hours, which is a whole evening. And dancing is very energetic and great fun. I also try to go swimming once or twice a week. It's good to relax after work, which is very stressful sometimes.

INTERVIEWER: Do you ever watch sport on TV?

ROISIN: No, never! People watch too much television. It's better to go out and do something! I hate sport on TV, especially football!

What do you think?

How much TV do students watch? What do they watch? When?

The words you need … to talk about sport

1
- Students can do this in pairs and then create questions to test the sporting knowledge of the others. Encourage them to ask questions beginning with *Who*? *What*? etc.
- Note that you *win* things: competitions, races, etc. and you *beat* people, other teams, etc.

Answers

1 lost   2 played / beat   3 won   4 beat   5 won

2 Ask students to do the exercise in pairs and to add to the examples in the box. Which do they like to do? Again, conduct a classroom survey or ask one of the students to do so.

Answers

play ice hockey, golf, football
do   (some / a lot of) running, yoga, aerobics, gymnastics, cycling, swimming, walking, weight training, skiing
go   running, cycling, swimming, walking, skiing

3 and 4

Students could do these alone, in pairs or as a whole group.

Answers

3 Football
   0 – 0   nil – nil
   1 – 0   one – nil

   1 – 1   one – all (one – one)
   2 – 1   two – one
Tennis
   15 – 0   fifteen – love
   15 – 15 fifteen – all
   30 – 15 thirty – fifteen
   40 – 40 deuce

4 A tennis match is decided by the winner of the bigger number of sets. Women usually play three sets and men play three or five sets. A set is won by reaching six games by two clear games or by winning 7 – 6 in a tie-break. In some matches, the last set is not decided by a tie-break and will continue until one player establishes a two-game lead. Note that 'game' can also sometimes mean 'match'.

It's time to talk

This could be a pairwork or serial pairwork activity. As students work on this, walk round helping pairs with vocabulary and taking notes to build up a list of sporting activities on the board. As part of your debriefing, you can try some collocation and vocabulary extension work on selected activities, for example football or tennis. Sometimes students can have a surprising grasp of the vocabulary of activities they like and it will be motivating for them if you can exploit this. On the other hand, you may have students who are not interested in either taking exercise or doing sport. You have to hope that they will agree with you that being able to discuss these subjects is an important area of conversation and worth working on if only for this reason.

What did we do today?

Check the Remember section quickly and remind students of the objectives of the lesson.

Follow up

Encourage students to:
1 write sentences about sport and physical activities and build up vocabulary lists around one or two selected activities which they would like to be able to talk about
2 make notes from films, TV or overheard conversations about how other people respond to different kinds of news.

13 Chanel

What did we do last time?

Do a review of the last type 1 lesson (Unit 10). Remind students of what they worked on and do some quick revision as follows.

Comparing things

- Ask students to make sentences comparing things or people using words like *tired*, *difficult*, *old*, *beautiful*, etc. to check the correct formation of the comparative form and their use of 'than'.

- To check the superlative, provide a model like: *The highest mountain / the longest river in this country is . . .* Then ask for sentences with the superlative forms of words like *old, new, interesting, ugly*, etc.

Weak stress
Write on the board sentences like:
- We're better than the rest.
- We're the best in the country.
- We're cheaper than they are.
- It's more difficult for us than it is for them.

Read them out and mark the stresses. Then rub out the stress marks and ask selected students to read them and mark the stresses.

On the agenda: Why are we doing this?
Tell students the objectives of this lesson:
- to learn how to use the **past simple** to talk about your past life
- to practise **pronouncing** the **past simple forms** of some regular verbs.

Reinforce this by writing the key words on the board or OHP.

Classroom language
Words to check for understanding before or during the unit are:

| irregular | regular | rule |

Warm up
- Ask students to describe what they see in the pictures. Do they like the fashions they see?
- Ask the Warm-up questions or get students to ask each other in pairs.
- Look at the picture of Coco Chanel and read the caption. Check understanding of 'designer' and ask how many people have heard of her. ('Do you know about this woman? Do you know her name?')

Listen to this

Gabrielle (Coco) Chanel – inventor of the fashion industry

Explain that we can use the past simple tense to talk about our past lives and the lives of others and that first of all they are going to listen to and then talk about details of the life of Coco Chanel.

1 Before playing track 13.1, students may benefit from practising saying dates – 1949, 1984, etc. You can play a quick game by asking them to identify famous people from their dates, e.g.
1564 – 1616 (William Shakespeare)
1769 – 1821 (Napoleon Bonaparte)
1685 – 1750 (Johann Sebastian Bach)
1475 – 1564 (Michelangelo)
1881 – 1973 (Pablo Picasso) etc.

Answers
1 a 1946   b 1971   c 1910   d 1924   e 1921   f 1883   g 1954

2 1 From the name of a song which she sang.
2 It was the fifth perfume they tested.
3 He held a fashion show for her.
4 She created the two-piece suit for women.

- After checking the answers, you could ask students what verbs in the past simple they have heard on the track and write them on the board in two unidentified groups: regular and irregular.
- Play the track again and ask them to note other verbs in the past simple. Check their results this time against the tapescript, ask what the two categories on the board represent and ask for the infinitive forms of the irregular forms.
- You could also ask them to reconstruct the story of Chanel's life from what they have heard and from the information on the page and on the board, either in pairs or as a whole group.

Track 13.1 tapescript ▶▶

INTERVIEWER: OK, Julie. Can you tell me a little bit about Coco Chanel? And first, the name. Why Coco?

JULIE: That's easy. The name Coco comes from a song she always sang, Cocorico, which became Coco.

INTERVIEWER: Tell us about her life.

JULIE: Well, she was born in France, in the Loire region, in 1883. The first important date is 1910 when she opened her first clothes shop, I think the name was Chanel Modes, Chanel Fashion in English.

INTERVIEWER: When did she launch the famous Chanel No. 5?

JULIE: Chanel No. 5? That was much later, in 1921. And I need to tell you about the name, why Chanel No. 5. It's very simple. They tested many perfumes, they didn't like the first four but number five was fantastic. And so, number five tested was the perfume they chose to sell, and so got the name Chanel No. 5.

INTERVIEWER: I see. And after that, what did she do?

JULIE: Well, she did a lot of things. One important thing, in 1924, she worked with Pierre and Paul Wertheimer to create Société des Parfums Chanel, which you can still find today. But it wasn't always a happy life.

INTERVIEWER: Why not?

JULIE: Well, she had some problems during the Second World War. She had some connections, some communication, with the Nazis and so she left France after the war and moved to Switzerland in 1946. She only returned to Paris in 1954. It was a long time before she had a good position again. In fact, Yves Saint Laurent held a fashion show for her in 1967 and this was the start of her comeback. It was very important for her.

INTERVIEWER: I know that she died in 1971. But you still see Chanel's influence today, especially with modern businesswomen.

JULIE: Oh, yes. Coco Chanel changed women's lives. She was the first designer to use the two-piece suit for women, to use men's clothes for women. And this was a big, big change at that time. And, I think it's very important to women today, especially in business. So, I think, wherever you go, you can still see the fashion of Coco Chanel.

What do you think?

You can ask students to assess the importance of clothes and fashion in their lives on a scale of 0 (not at all) to 5 (extremely) and do a quick classroom survey.

Check your grammar

The past simple

Check the extent of students' knowledge:
- Ask for the past simple form of some common regular and irregular verbs.
- Give them some simple statements in the past simple (e.g. *They went to New York last week, They had a good time, She played really well*) and ask them to convert them into questions.
- Give them some more simple statements in the past simple and ask them to convert them into negatives.
- Ask for similar manipulations for the verb *to be* (*We were happy once, You were in the army before*).

Now ask students to complete the gaps alone or in pairs. Check the answers.

Answers
1 was 2 weren't 3 wasn't 4 Were 5 did 6 arrived
7 didn't 8 got 9 went 10 had

Do it yourself

1

Answers
1 I did it yesterday.
2 I didn't have time.
3 Were you busy?
4 What did you do last night?

Background briefing: Stella McCartney

Stella McCartney was born in 1971, the daughter of ex-Beatle Sir Paul and Linda McCartney. She graduated from London's Central St Martin's College of Art & Design in 1995 with a show featuring supermodels Naomi Campbell and Kate Moss modelling her clothes. In 1997 she was appointed chief designer at the French couture house Chloe and her first collection for the house, shown in Paris in October 1997, quickly dispelled any doubts about her talent. She launched her own fashion house in 2001 under her name in partnership with Gucci.

Following the death of her mother in April 1998, Stella stepped up her fight against the maltreatment of animals, a cause Linda had always held dear. A month later, during Fur Fashion Week, she teamed up with PETA (People for the Ethical Treatment of Animals) to release a video championing animal rights.

2 Ask students what they know about Stella McCartney (see above) before reading the text and writing the correct forms. Check the answers and start checking that students are remembering key irregular forms now.

Answers
1 was 2 started 3 left 4 didn't want 5 graduated
6 joined 7 stayed 8 left 9 launched 10 were

3 Students can do this in pairs before asking each other the same questions and thinking of others which you can write on the board during the feedback.

Answers
1 was 2 grow 3 did 4 study 5 join 6 long 7 stay

4 Ask students to do the exercise and read the dialogue in pairs. Can they think of other questions in the past simple which are useful in social conversation? Play track 13.2 for students to check their answers.

Answers
1 do 2 went 3 did 4 was 5 wasn't 6 didn't

Track 13.2 tapescript

GENEVIEVE: Afternoon, Peter. You look tired! What did you do last night?
PETER: Hi, I went to a restaurant for an early dinner and then to the cinema.
GENEVIEVE: What did you see?
PETER: A Russian film. It was about a family in Moscow. I don't remember the title.
GENEVIEVE: Was it good?
PETER: No, it wasn't. I didn't understand it really.

Sounds good

The past simple

1 to 3

Proceed as indicated in the book and play tracks 13.3, 13.4 and 13.5 as indicated. Alternatively, if students have not already looked at this part of their books, you could work on eliciting the rules from them on the basis of examples:
- Ask them to close the book and get them to give you the past simple form of some regular verbs.
- Write the verbs they give you on the board in the three categories without labelling them. If necessary, add a few to each list.
- Then ask students why you have divided them into three groups. If they don't see the reason, ask them to read the verbs out, group by group.
- When they have understood the principle, proceed with exercises 1 and 2.

Answers

/t/	/d/	/ɪd/
liked	enjoyed	decided
decreased	received	wanted
looked	listened	visited
increased		
talked		
walked		

Tracks 13.3, 13.4 and 13.5 tapescripts
See Student's Book.

It's time to talk

The objective here is for students to find out about each other's past experiences. Students can work in pairs but, time permitting, with more than one other student so that during the feedback you can build up a picture of the background to individuals from more than one source.

What did we do today?
Check the Remember section quickly and remind students of the objectives of this lesson.

Follow up
Encourage students to:
1 write sentences about the past lives of themselves, friends and colleagues using the past simple
2 write a story in the past simple about a typical day, a very untypical day, a holiday or an important event in their life.

14 Médecins Sans Frontières

When looking at the unit title, students may be interested to know that the translation from the French is 'Doctors without borders'.

What did we do last time?
Do a review of the last type 2 lesson (Unit 11). Remind students of what they worked on (see Teacher's notes for that unit) and do some quick revision as follows.

Talking about your work
Ask selected students questions like:
- What do you do?
- Where do you work?
- What do you like about your job?

Now ask students to ask you (thus remembering and repeating) the same questions.

Structuring emails
Ask students to tell you the main parts of an email as given in Unit 11 (Greeting, Reason for writing, Action point and Close) and suggest possible phrases for each stage.

On the agenda: Why are we doing this?
Tell students the objectives of this lesson:
- to talk about **organisations and organisational structure**
- to practise **welcoming visitors** to your place of work. (You could remind them that in Unit 8 we looked at the situation of meeting a visitor at the airport.)

Reinforce this by writing the key words on the board or OHP.

Background briefing: Charities
This basic information comes from the websites of the four organisations mentioned in the Warm up.

Médecins Sans Frontières   Médecins Sans Frontières (MSF) is an international humanitarian aid organisation that provides emergency medical assistance to populations in danger in more than 80 countries. MSF works in rehabilitation of hospitals and dispensaries, vaccination programmes and water and sanitation projects. MSF also works in remote health care centres and slum areas and provides training of local personnel. All this is done with the objective of rebuilding health structures to acceptable levels.

Plan   Plan is an international humanitarian organisation helping children to realise their full potential. Plan was founded in 1937 in response to the plight of children left orphaned and destitute by the Spanish Civil War. Since then it has grown to help children in need in 45 developing countries. Plan works with people across the globe so that children in the poorest countries can change their world. It works long-term with children, their families and communities to build a world where children know and can claim their rights, and, where they are safe, healthy, and capable of realising their full potential. Plan is able to do this because a million people across the world sponsor a child and give a hand-up to entire communities.

WWF (formerly known as the World Wildlife Fund)   WWF's mission is to stop the degradation of the planet's natural environment and to build a future in which humans live in harmony with nature, by:
- conserving the world's biological diversity
- ensuring that the use of renewable natural sources is sustainable
- promoting the reduction of pollution and wasteful consumption.

Its work covers many different areas, from policy work to campaigning, on-the-ground action to education and capacity building.

Oxfam   Oxfam International is a confederation of 12 organisations working together in more than 100 countries to find lasting solutions to poverty, suffering and injustice. With many of the causes of poverty global in nature, members of Oxfam International believe they can achieve greater impact in addressing issues of poverty by their collective efforts. To achieve the maximum impact on poverty, Oxfam links up their work on development programmes and humanitarian response, lobbying for policy changes at national and global level. Its campaigns and communications work is aimed at mobilising public opinion for change.

You can get more information about each from: www.msf.org; www.plan-uk.org; www.panda.org; www.oxfam.org.

Warm up
Write these four key words or phrases on the board and ask students to match them with the four organisations:
- Children (to match Plan)
- Environment (WWF)
- Health (MSF)
- Food aid (Oxfam)

This is obviously an over-simplification of the work of each charity, though the key words do highlight a special area of concern of each.

Look at the picture of Polly and read the caption. Explain that in this unit they are going to read about how Médecins Sans Frontières is organised.

Read on

Médecins Sans Frontières – working to help people

1

> **Answers**
>
> 1 D   2 A   3 C   4 B

2 After checking the answers, ask one or two more questions to check general understanding and understanding of particular words, especially:
- centralised/decentralised
- based in
- department.

Ask students to make sentences about their own organisations using these words.

> **Answers**
>
> 1 Over 30 years ago
> 2 Gives medical help to people in wars and natural disasters. It also tells the world about them.
> 3 The three centres are in Brussels, Paris and Barcelona but they also work in 85 other countries.
> 4 She communicates important information about medicine to people in India and Africa.

What do you think?

Ask students for the reasons for their answers.

The words you need ... to talk about your organisation

1 It is worth spending some time on both exercises, particularly on the transfers (where they talk about their own organisations), since it is important for students to be able to describe their own organisations, even in simple terms. Check the answers, then go round the class and ask each student to provide sentences about his/her own organisation. If students work for different organisations, go round the class for each sentence in the exercise.

> **Answers**
>
> 1 started   2 headquarters   3 based   4 offices   5 active
> 6 department

2 Ask them if they can think of other companies or organisations which they can make sentences about, for each of the verbs in the box.

> **Answers**
>
> 1 gives   2 publishes   3 supplies   4 makes   5 sells
> 6 provides

It's time to talk

- Organise pairs and ask students to look at their respective file cards.

- Ask students to prepare questions. You might like to have all the As and Bs working together but in two separate groups at this stage.
- Note that there are two or three questions they could ask under 'Other information'.

COMMUNICATING AT WORK

Visiting an organisation

Explain that this part of the unit is about language for receiving visitors. Start by asking:
- how many people in the class receive visitors and how often – in their own language and in English
- how many of them make visits to other organisations – in their own language and in English
- how visitors like to be received – what makes a good welcome?
- what phrases they might use to welcome a visitor in English – at reception, and in someone's office.

> **Answers**
>
> **1** 1 appointment   2 tell   3 sign   4 course   5 moment
> 6 could   7 badge

Track 14.1 tapescript ▶▶

KEIKO: Good morning. My name's Keiko Sumi. I've got an appointment with Patrick Hart at 10 o'clock.
RECEPTIONIST: Just a moment, Ms Sumi. I'll tell him you're here. Could you sign the visitors' book?
KEIKO: Of course.
RECEPTIONIST: Right. Mr Hart will be with you in a moment.
KEIKO: Thank you.
RECEPTIONIST: And could you put on this security badge, please?

> **Answers**
>
> **4** Nice to meet you.
> Please follow me.
> Is this your first trip to London?
> Here we are.
> Please take a seat.
> Can I get you a drink?
> 250 people work in this building.

Track 14.2 tapescript ▶▶

PATRICK: Hello, Patrick Hart. Nice to meet you.
KEIKO: Hello, Keiko Sumi. Nice to meet you.
PATRICK: Please follow me. We can go to my office.
KEIKO: Great.
PATRICK: And is this your first trip to London?
KEIKO: No, I've been here twice before. .
PATRICK: So, here we are. Please take a seat.
KEIKO: Thank you.
PATRICK: Can I get you a drink? Tea, coffee …
KEIKO: Coffee would be great.
PATRICK: No problem.
KEIKO: So, how many people work here?
PATRICK: 250 people work in this building. It's our headquarters.
KEIKO: I see.

5 Read through the information with the students. You may like to ask them to give you examples of language required at each stage before they start the pairwork exercise.

What did we do today?
Check the Remember section quickly and remind students of the objectives of this lesson.

Follow up
Encourage students to:
1 write six or more sentences about their own organisation
2 write down key phrases for visiting an organisation or receiving visitors to an organisation.

15 Trekking in Nepal

What did we do last time?
Do a review of the last type 3 lesson (Unit 12). Remind students of what they worked on (see Teacher's notes for that unit) and do some quick revision as follows.

Responding to news
Ask students for useful phrases for responding to good news, interesting news, bad news and surprising news.

Words for sport and physical exercise
Ask students to tell you:
- two or three things in relation to sport and physical exercise that they love doing and hate doing in their free time
- the difference between *win* and *beat*
- two or three sports or activities that collocate with *do*, *go* and *play*
- a football score and a tennis score.

On the agenda: Why are we doing this?
Tell students the objectives of this lesson:
- to practise useful **phrases for air travel**
- to learn and practise **vocabulary for holidays and travel**.
Reinforce this by writing the key words on the board or OHP.

Warm up
Ask students to describe the backdrop photo (where is it?) and briefly to answer the Warm-up questions. You can start a list of types of holiday on the board: *beach*, *touring*, *cruising*, *cultural*, *specialist*, etc.

Getting there

> **Answers**
> 1 c 2 e 3 j 4 f 5 d 6 h 7 b 8 i 9 a 10 g

Track 15.1 tapescript ▶▶
Checking in
A: Can I check in here for Vienna?
B: Yes. Can I see your passport and ticket, please?
A: Of course.
B: Would you prefer a window or an aisle seat?
A: An aisle seat, please.
B: Boarding is at 17.30 at gate 45.

Getting information at the gate
A: Excuse me, do you have any information about the Amsterdam flight?
B: Yes, the flight is delayed by 45 minutes.
A: OK, so when is boarding?
B: Boarding is now at 18.30. I'm very sorry for the delay.

On the plane
A: Excuse me, could you put your bag in the overhead locker?
B: They're full. There's no room.
A: Can you put it under your seat?
B: OK, I'll do that.
A: Thank you.

Arriving without luggage
A: Hello, my suitcase didn't arrive.
B: Right, I need some information from you.
A: OK, this is my flight information and a local address.
B: Thank you. You're very organised.
A: Yes, this isn't the first time!

Have a go
You can ask them to think of another situation connected with air travel so that the others have to guess what it is when they hear the dialogue.

Listen to this
Walking at 5,000 metres
1
- Look at the photo of Jürgen and read the rubric. What's the difference between walking and trekking? (Answer: Trekking is harder!) Do any students go trekking? Where? Alone or as a member of an organised group?
- You could also ask them to offer answers to the questions in exercise 2 before listening to track 15.2 for the first time.

> **Answers**
> **1** When: 10 years ago
> Number of days walking: 25 days
> Distance walked every day: 18 kilometres
> Size of trekking group: 2
>
> **2** 1 The air was very thin so sometimes there wasn't enough oxygen
> 2 Rucksack, sleeping bag and warm clothing
> 3 Rice, potatoes, vegetables
> 4 The walking, the exercise, the countryside, the clean air and the quiet

Track 15.2 tapescript ▶▶|

INTERVIEWER: So, Jürgen. Tell me about your best holiday.
JÜRGEN: Well, it was definitely my trekking holiday in Nepal.
INTERVIEWER: OK. When did you go?
JÜRGEN: I went to Nepal about 10 years ago on a trekking tour, to do some walking in the mountains.
INTERVIEWER: How long did you go for?
JÜRGEN: The trekking tour was about 25 days from Kathmandu to very close to the Everest base camp.
INTERVIEWER: 25 days! That's a long time. How far did you walk every day?
JÜRGEN: That's quite difficult. Not really far, I think. Perhaps, 18 kilometres. But you have to climb up and down a lot every day.
INTERVIEWER: So, it was very hard trekking?
JÜRGEN: Yeah, very hard trekking. Sometimes, you have problems walking at only five thousand metres where the air is very thin, and you have a lot of problems with not enough oxygen.
INTERVIEWER: What kind of equipment did you take with you?
JÜRGEN: Not much. Only a rucksack, a sleeping bag and some warm clothing and that's all. There's a lot of lodges and so equipment is not a problem. But you need a good sleeping bag to keep out the cold, believe me.
INTERVIEWER: And how was the food?
JÜRGEN: Good. There was a lot of rice and in the higher mountains a lot of potatoes and only a few vegetables, normally no beef, no meat. But it was good, very good.
INTERVIEWER: How many people were you walking with?
JÜRGEN: I was travelling only with my wife so there were just two of us. And we carried all our things by ourselves, so no porters. We saw some people at night in the lodges but during the day we walked alone.
INTERVIEWER: What was the best thing about the trip?
JÜRGEN: The walking and the exercise. I hate holidays where you sit and sunbathe. I like to be out in the countryside, and in Nepal, at four or five thousand metres, it's perfect. The air is very clean, it's very quiet, it's just a beautiful place. You must go!

What do you think?

Ask students briefly if they have had experiences of any other kinds of adventure holiday, e.g. white water rafting, sky diving, etc.

The words you need ... for holidays and travel

1 After the exercise, ask them to cover their books. Give them the verbs in the box as cues, and ask them to make sentences about holidays with the verbs – either to reproduce the ones in the book from memory or to produce something original.

> **Answers**
> 1 Do   2 Go   3 Sit   4 Hire   5 Relax   6 Take

2 You can ask supplementary transfer questions based on the sentences in this exercise like:
  1 How do you normally travel on holiday? (by car? coach? plane?)
  3 What's the biggest delay you've ever had on a plane? etc.
Keep building up additional vocabulary on the board.

> **Answers**
> 1 by   2 took   3 late   4 rank   5 trolley   6 attendant
> 7 missed   8 flight

It's time to talk

- Manage this as a serial pairwork exercise. Students should first work on their own to write details of a good holiday they once had and also to prepare questions for their partners before they get up and circulate.
- The feedback session should give you some interesting information on your students' ideas about great holiday locations. Use the debriefing to consolidate the vocabulary you've covered in this lesson.

What did we do today?

Check the Remember section quickly and remind students of the objectives of this lesson.

Follow up

Encourage students to:
1 write a short account of a holiday
2 read English language holiday brochures for gist to get more vocabulary for different types of holiday and to add to the Places section in their vocabulary notebooks.

Revision 1 Units 1–15

Answers

Grammar

1
1 What do you do?
2 Which company do you work for?
3 Where does she come from?
4 Do you do much sport at the weekend?
5 What did you do last night?
6 What did you have to eat?
7 Did you have a good trip?
8 How long did it take to get here?

2
1 Are there a lot of restaurants near your office? / Is there a restaurant near your office?
2 Is there a lot of information on your website?
3 Are there a lot of people who need English for their job?
4 I think English grammar is easier than Russian grammar.
5 Gucci clothes are generally more expensive than clothes from Marks & Spencer.
6 I think the weather today is worse than yesterday.

General vocabulary

1 quiet – noisy
clean – dirty
empty – full
safe – dangerous
beautiful – ugly
low – high

2 1 relax   2 do   3 go   4 play   5 get   6 drive

Business communication

1 1 speak   2 Who's   3 put   4 can   5 calling   6 See

2 1 Dear   2 send   3 Attached   4 information
5 contact / call   6 Best

Pronunciation

1 1 We have a message for you.
2 It's about our company.
3 It's a great place to work.
4 We need another 50 people.
5 So come and join us.

Track R1.1 tapescript ▶▶
See Student's Book.

2

/t/	/d/	/ɪd/
liked	played	needed
decreased	enjoyed	decided
looked	listened	visited
walked		

Track R1.2 tapescript ▶▶
played   needed   liked   decreased   decided
looked   enjoyed   listened   walked   visited

Business vocabulary

1 1 offices   2 industry   3 started   4 headquarters
5 based   6 responsible

2 1 customer   2 employer   3 competitor   4 employee
5 supplier   6 consultant

Social phrases

1 1 d   2 e   3 a   4 c   5 b   6 f

2 *Possible answers*
1 How are you?
2 Could I have a receipt, please? / Could you give me a receipt, please?
3 Would you like some/a coffee?
4 Keep the change.
5 How much is this/that?
6 Have a good weekend.

16 Project Stockholm

What did we do last time?
Do a review of the last type 1 lesson (Unit 13). Remind students of what they worked on (see Teacher's notes for that unit) and do some quick revision as follows.

The past simple
Ask students to tell you something about:
- the past lives
- the recent past (what they did last weekend, the last film someone saw, etc.)
of other people in the class.

You can also play a quick true/false game. Tell students two things about your past, one true and one false, using the past simple tense in both cases. Students have to guess which is which. Ask them to do the same.

Pronunciation
- Write up on the board one example of each type of pronunciation of the past simple, e.g. *managed*, *talked* and *presented*.
- Ask them for more regular verbs in the past simple and ask them to pronounce them too and tell you which category to write them in; or
- Tell them the infinitive forms of other regular verbs and ask selected students to give you the pronunciation and to tell you which column to write them in.

On the agenda: Why are we doing this?
Tell students the objectives of this lesson:
- to practise using the **present continuous** to talk about temporary situations
- pronunciation – **sentence stress** – to learn about how stress works in sentences.

Reinforce this by writing the key words on the board or OHP.

Classroom language
A word to check for understanding before or during the unit is:

| temporary |

Warm up
- Ask the questions in the present continuous and elicit answers in the same tense. You may need to provide model answers yourself, e.g. *I'm working on a new course at the moment*. Emphasise 'at the moment'!
- Look at the photo of Riggert and read the caption. Explain to students that they are going to hear about a project he is working on at the moment too.

Unit sixteen **49**

Listen to this

What project are you working on at the moment?

1

Answers
Number of workers: 200
Location: Stockholm city centre
Architect: Norman Foster
Project: Building a new bridge

2 After checking the answers, look at the grammar of the true/false statements:
- Point out the forms of the verb in this exercise.
- Can students find the negative?
- Can they convert the statements into questions?
- Can they identify the differences between the present simple and the present continuous?
- Can they say what the main uses are for the present simple? and the continuous?

Answers
1 T   2 F   3 T   4 F

Track 16.1 tapescript ▶▶

INTERVIEWER: So, what is your name and what do you do?
RIGGERT: My name is Riggert Andersson and I'm a project manager working for the Swedish Railroad Authority. I have about 200 people working in the projects that I am managing.
INTERVIEWER: What project are you working on at the moment?
RIGGERT: At the moment, we have two big projects and with both projects the idea is to have more railroad capacity into Stockholm and through Stockholm. My project is a new bridge called Årstabron, more or less in the city centre.
INTERVIEWER: OK, and who designed the bridge?
RIGGERT: Sir Norman Foster designed it. He won an international competition and we are very happy with it.
INTERVIEWER: What is so good about his design?
RIGGERT: It's perfect for the environment. This is a very sensitive part of Stockholm and there is already a bridge in that area. But the new bridge goes with both very well.
INTERVIEWER: So you have to be very sensitive to those kinds of environmental issues?
RIGGERT: Yes, absolutely. When you build anything in Sweden, it's very important to think about the environment.
INTERVIEWER: What exactly are you working on at the moment, which part of the bridge?
RIGGERT: We are working on the foundations and the pillars and want to start with the top part of the bridge soon.
INTERVIEWER: Are you enjoying it?
RIGGERT: Very much indeed, it's a very interesting job. It has everything; it's not only a technical job, it's also a job with a lot of other things. I work a lot with local people. I'm talking and listening all the time to people living close to the railroad, giving information and so on. I like that part of the job.
INTERVIEWER: And are you speaking a lot of English in the project at the moment?
RIGGERT: Not very much at the moment. We have some groups coming to visit the project from other countries and then we use English as the main language. It's increasing and when we get further into the project there will be more.

What do you think?

Quickly collect a few examples of environmentally friendly work from the country or region of each student.

Check your grammar

The present continuous 1

Look at the three different uses of the present continuous. Give them your own examples for each category. Then ask students to:
1 say what they're doing at the moment
2 make a sentence about a current project (which can be a repeat of the Warm up, if necessary)
3 make a statement about a current trend or development – in the country, in the organisation where they work, in the weather, etc.

Now:
- Ask students to complete the gaps in this section, then check the answers.
- Check the students' pronunciation of the contracted forms.
- Read the note. There are other uses for the present continuous and also there are certain verbs which are normally used in the present simple rather than the present continuous – see the sections on the present continuous and present simple in the Grammar reference section in the Student's Book.

Answers
1 are   2 working   3 not   4 is   5 staying   6 is   7 aren't
8 not   9 am   10 not

Do it yourself

1 to 3

As you check the answers, ask students to explain why they have chosen one tense rather than another. Play track 16.2 for students to listen and check before you check exercise 3.

Students can also read this dialogue in pairs and role-play mini-dialogues as a follow up to exercise 3 based on questions like: *What are you reading at the moment?*

Answers

1
JANE: Where are you staying this week? In a hotel?
RIGGERT: Yes, I'm staying in a little hotel near the conference centre.
JANE: So, are you enjoying the conference?
RIGGERT: No, I'm not enjoying it. I hate conferences!

2 1 designs; are designing   2 produces
3 are launching   4 am running   5 work; are working

3 1 are you working on
2 are/'re reorganising
3 isn't working
4 am/'m working
5 don't like
6 are/'re developing
7 are travelling
8 go

Track 16.2 tapescript ▶▶

HELGE: Hi, Lars. What are you working on at the moment?
LARS: I'm so busy. We're reorganising the department right now and it's a lot of work.
HELGE: Really? Where's Anita?
LARS: Anita isn't working this week. She's on holiday. What about you? Are you busy?
HELGE: Very busy. I'm working on a new marketing project.
LARS: Really, but you always say you don't like marketing!
HELGE: Yeah, but actually, this project is quite interesting. We're developing a new sun cream.
LARS: Does the market need another sun cream?
HELGE: Oh, yes. More and more people are travelling abroad these days.
LARS: Lucky people. I never go on holiday – I don't have the time.

Sounds good

Sentence stress

1 Ask the question and ask students to read the three sentences to help them get the answer. Then play track 16.3 and ask the question again. Can any of them explain why the three sentences take about the same time to say, before they read the explanation? Ask students to invent other similar examples.

Answers

All three sentences can take about the same time to say.

2 You can ask students to read the dialogue before and after they hear track 16.4. Encourage them to really accentuate the accented syllables to the point of exaggeration.

Answers

A: Are you <u>working</u> from <u>home</u> <u>next</u> <u>week</u>?
B: <u>Yes</u>, I'm <u>working</u> from <u>home</u> to the <u>end</u> of the <u>month</u>.
A: Are you <u>busy</u>?
B: <u>Yes</u>, but I'm <u>enjoying</u> the <u>work</u>.

3 Ask students to work in pairs, and, again, insist on quite heavy accentuation (in the right places!).
  Ask students to provide their own questions and answers in the present continuous and to practise saying them aloud.

Answers

2 Are you reading a good book at the moment?
3 Are you enjoying the lesson?
4 What are you doing?
5 Are you having a good time?

Tracks 16.3 and 16.4 tapescript ▶▶
See Student's Book.

It's time to talk

Handle this in the normal way for file cards (see Introduction page 16). Make sure students take notes during the exercise.

What did we do today?
Check the Remember section quickly and remind students of the objectives of this lesson.

Follow up
Encourage students to:
1 write sentences about a photograph or other image, describing in the present continuous what is happening in the picture
2 record some short passages of authentic English and practise replicating the stress patterns of simple sentences as accurately as they can.

17 Workplace communication

What did we do last time?
Do a review of the last type 2 lesson (Unit 14). Remind students of what they worked on (see Teacher's notes for that unit) and do some quick revision as follows.

Organisations
Ask selected students to tell you about:
- when their organisation was started
- where the head office is
- what its main activities are
- what the main departments are.

Ask them to make sentences about their organisations using one or more of these verbs:
sells makes supplies buys

Welcoming visitors
Ask students to make complete sentences used for welcoming visitors, using these key words:
- Welcome (e.g. Welcome to the head office of Siemens.)
- Nice   (e.g. Nice to meet you.)
- follow   (e.g. Please follow me.)
- seat   (e.g. Please take a seat.)
- hope   (e.g. I hope you have a nice stay.)
- drink   (e.g. Can I get you a drink?)

On the agenda: Why are we doing this?
Tell students the objectives of this lesson:
- to talk about **communication at work** and what makes a good communicator
- to learn **communication verbs**
- to practise **replying to emails**.
Reinforce this by writing the key words on the board or OHP.

Background briefing
This unit begins with a text about video-conferencing. This is a cost-saving way of organising a meeting without all the participants travelling to the same place to meet. Instead they go to a room with the technical facilities to transmit

Unit seventeen 51

sound and images of the participants to similarly equipped offices in other locations. Problems can therefore arise if the equipment does not function properly, for example, because the telecoms link is poor. Poor turn-taking during the meeting can also create problems, particularly if there are a lot of participants and especially for those who are not using their native language.

Classroom language

A word to check for understanding before or during the unit is:

> communication

Warm up

- Ask students to make sentences about the different forms of communication in the pictures by asking in each case: *What is he / is she / are they doing?* (to encourage students to use the present continuous and the appropriate verb in each case).
- Ask them to answer the two questions. Can they name other forms of communication?
- Ask them to look at the photo of Paula and to read the caption. Check understanding of *publishing*.

Read on

Communication of the future

1 Students should read questions 1 to 4 and can, if you like, give their own short answers, before reading the four paragraphs. Then check their matches and ask them to answer the four questions. You can also ask:
  - how many different forms of communication are mentioned in the text (answer: five or six – depending on whether you count face-to-face communication separately: meetings, talking via the Internet, telephoning, emailing, face-to-face communication, video-conferencing)
  - how many different communication verbs are used in the text (answers may vary – does *interrupt* qualify? – but the main ones are: *meet, talk, speak, discuss, ask, explain, listen.* Students need not worry about not understanding all of them straightaway. You'll be looking at verbs like this during the lesson.

> **Answers**
> 1 C   2 A   3 D   4 B

2 After the exercise, ask them how many people they think can take part in a successful video-conference. (There isn't a necessarily correct answer to this: it depends on the quality of the technical link and on how disciplined the participants are in signalling that they wish to make a contribution, but generally speaking, the smaller the number the better, from a purely communications point of view.)

> **Answers**
> 1 For marketing meetings
> 2 There is a delay with the voice, so you wait after people speak to hear the words
> 3 Because it's face-to-face and therefore more personal
> 4 You have to buy a lot of equipment

What do you think?

Which forms of communication do they prefer? For example, do they prefer telephone or email? Do any of them prefer video-conferencing (or the idea of it) to face-to-face communication?

The words you need ... to talk about communication

Explain that video-conferencing is one form of professional communication and that you are now going to look at the vocabulary of communication in general.

1 Students can do this exercise on their own and then take it in turns to test each other.

> **Answers**
> 1 talk   2 explain   3 ask   4 interrupt   5 listening
> 6 contact   7 call

2 Students can do this alone or in pairs. Emphasise to them how important it is to get the prepositions right with these verbs and aim to recycle this work frequently until students have learnt the correct forms.

> **Answers**
> 1 discuss   2 speaks   3 listens to   4 replies to   5 reads
> 6 calls   7 asks   8 interrupts

It's time to talk

- Explain to students that you want them to talk about the qualities of the ideal manager as a communicator in this exercise and that they should draw their ideas in part from the previous exercise.
- Do a quick class survey during the debriefing. Are the points they've made relevant only to managers or to anyone who works with other people?

COMMUNICATING AT WORK

Emails 2: Replying to emails

Check understanding of the different forms of address (Mr, Mrs, etc.). Explain that Ms is a form used by women more in writing than in speaking as an equivalent to Mr, i.e. it does not show if the person is married or not. Always use Ms when you are writing professionally to a woman for the first time whose preferred form of address you do not know.

1 Before they start, ask them:
  - to remind you of the main parts of an email and ask for examples of greetings and closes
  - how they typically begin a reply to any email they

receive. (For example: *Thanks for your mail. / Thanks for your email. / Thanks for your email dated 9 January*, etc.)

Answers
1 Greeting: Hi Jan
2 Polite beginning: Thanks for your email and the attached report.
3 Information/Action point: I'll read it over the weekend and call you on Monday.
4 Close: Enjoy the weekend.

2 After doing the exercise, you could also ask them to write or suggest additional sentences to follow the ones in the Student's Book in an email, for example: Nice to hear from you and great news that you're coming. I will book a table at your favourite restaurant for the evening after the meeting. / Thanks for the report. It looks excellent.

Answers
1 d   2 a   3 b   4 c

3 If available, a computer or overhead projector may be useful for group feedback.

Possible answers
Dear Sam
Here is another copy of the report I sent last week.
Best wishes
Frank

Dear Adrian
Klara has told me that you have kindly passed on a possible new customer for me, John Peters. I am very grateful and will contact John soon.
Kind regards
Frank

What did we do today?
Check the Remember section quickly and remind students of the objectives of this lesson.

Follow up
Encourage students to:
1 write sentences using the communication verbs in this unit
2 keep a record of emails they write in English to show you and the rest of the class.

18 Slow food

What did we do last time?
Do a review of the last type 3 lesson (Unit 15). Remind students of what they worked on (see Teacher's notes for that unit) and do some quick revision as follows.

Air travel
Ask students to give you complete phrases containing these words: *check in, passport, window seat, gate, delayed, boarding, overhead locker.*

Holidays and travel
Ask the class to tell you 10 or 12 different things you can do on holiday. Write their responses on the board. You might elicit responses like:
- You can visit a museum
- You can go on a coach tour
- You can sunbathe on the beach, etc.

On the agenda: Why are we doing this?
Tell students the objectives of this lesson:
- to practise useful phrases for eating **in the restaurant**
- to learn and practise **food and drink** vocabulary.

Reinforce this by writing the key words on the board or OHP.

Background briefing: Slow Food
Slow Food is an international movement for the protection not only of taste in food, but of a way of life associated with pleasure, good food, the survival of endangered foods, and so on: members call themselves 'eco-gastronomes'. It was started in Italy in 1986 and Italy accounts for half of its 60,000 plus worldwide membership today. The movement became an international one in Paris in 1989 and now has branches all over the world. It publishes a magazine called 'Slow' in five languages. For more information, go to www.slowfood.com

Warm up
- Ask students the questions. Ask them what kind of restaurants their favourites are (French, Chinese, Italian, etc.). You can brainstorm a list of favourite national cuisines on the board.
- Ask what foods they can see in the backdrop photo. (Answer: melon, peach, grapes, cauliflower, apples, watermelon, carrots, bananas, lemons, tomatoes, peppers, courgettes, strawberries, sweetcorn, and more. (You will ask them about Slow Food after the dialogues.)
- Explain that not only is knowing food and restaurant vocabulary useful for travellers but that it's important to be able to translate menus into English when entertaining visitors to your own country. This unit will help them develop both these skills.

Restaurant talk

Answers

1 i 2 b 3 d 4 f 5 e 6 h 7 j 8 a 9 g 10 c

Track 18.1 tapescript ▶▶

At the restaurant

A: Good evening. I have a reservation. My name's Brillakis.
B: Yes, the table by the window. Can I take your coats?
A: Thank you.
C: Thanks.
B: So, the menu and the wine list. Would you like a drink before you order?

Before the meal

B: Are you ready to order?
C: Yes. We'll both have the pâté as a starter, please. What's John Dory?
B: John Dory is a kind of white sea fish.
C: Then I'll have the John Dory.
A: The salmon, please.
B: Right. And to drink?
A: We'll have a bottle of the house white.

During the meal

B: Is everything all right?
C: Yes, thanks. Oh, can I have some more bread, please?
B: Sure. And would you like some more wine?
A: No, thanks. Actually, could we have a bottle of sparkling mineral water?

After the meal

B: So, did you enjoy your meal?
C: Yes, thank you. It was very nice.
B: Good. And would you like anything else? More coffee?
C: No, thank you. Could we have the bill, please?
B: Of course.

Have a go

Can Students invent other short dialogues set in the restaurant?

Listen to this

A great place to eat

1 Look at the picture of Wendy and ask the question about Slow Food (see Background briefing on page 53). Then look at the five statements under 'Slow Food movement' and ask about or explain *intensive farming*.

Answers

1   1 was established in Italy in 1986
    2 became international in 1989
    3 is against intensive farming
    4 prefers food which is local and simple
    5 wants to see good service in restaurants

2   1 The movement was started after the opening of a McDonald's restaurant in Rome, Italy.
    2 Wendy thinks that intensive farming is bad for animals, bad for the taste of meat, and maybe bad for our health.
    3 From local producers
    4 Slow means good – good **food** and good **service**.

Track 18.2 tapescript ▶▶

INTERVIEWER: So, what is Slow Food?
WENDY: Well, the Slow Food idea began in 1986. In that year, McDonald's opened a fast food restaurant in a very historic piazza in Rome. This was terrible. So, many people wanted to create an organisation to promote traditional Italian food and Italian food culture.
INTERVIEWER: But the movement is now international?
WENDY: Yes, it is. The movement became international in 1989. There was a congress in Paris on 14th July, Bastille Day, and now the organisation has 65,000 members in 45 countries around the world.
INTERVIEWER: And why do so many people like the idea of Slow Food?
WENDY: Many people don't like fast food or mass-produced food because it needs cheap meat, which means a lot of intensive, very industrial farming. And intensive farming is bad for animals, bad for the taste of meat, and may be bad for us. Think about the problems with meat in England over the last few years.
INTERVIEWER: OK and what for you is a good restaurant?
WENDY: I think the most important thing is that the ingredients are local, you know, where possible. We like a restaurant to promote local food. We also love it when a menu is simple. We think you can have some great flavours by making the dishes as simple as possible.
INTERVIEWER: Do you have a favourite restaurant?
WENDY: Yes, in London there's a restaurant called St John with a chef called Fergus Henderson. He's a very instinctive cook. He gets his products from local producers he knows. And, with him, you can have a very basic dish and it will taste fantastic because it is so simple and the quality of the products is so great. So I think that's probably one of my favourites.
INTERVIEWER: Are there any other reasons that you like this restaurant?
WENDY: I think it's very friendly, all of the staff know about food and about wine, they are all very well trained. And that's another important thing for Slow Food. We believe fast food means lower quality of food and lower quality of service. Slow means good – good food and good service.

What do you think?

Do students think all fast food is bad? What do their children or young people they know think? Why do people eat fast food? What do they think about the Slow Food movement? Do they want to become members?

The words you need ... for eating and drinking

1 After students have done this exercise, ask them to show you what they understand by *plate* and to give you examples of the other words in the box. For famous dishes, ask them: *If a visitor to your country could eat just one national dish, which dish would you choose for him or her? Can you describe it?*

Answers

1 dish 2 plate 3 starter 4 dessert 5 cuisine

2 Students can work in pairs or perhaps in groups of three or four in a bigger class. This exercise may generate a lot

of vocabulary, so be ready to spend some time collecting additional words and phrases during the feedback. Note that some terms, like John Dory, are deliberately obscure. Students should be able to deduce what it is and be able to explain to others (*It's a kind of fish*) as part of the skill of dealing with food and drink.

Answers

1 meat 2 seafood 3 fish 4 vegetables 5 fruit 6 drinks

It's time to talk

Students can play this game in pairs, or you can create groups of three and nominate one of them to referee. If there is disagreement, students can check the language presented in the unit or appeal to you.

During feedback, ask the class to agree on definitive expressions for each box in the game.

What did we do today?

Check the Remember section quickly and remind students of the objectives of this lesson.

Follow up

Encourage students to:
1 start another theme-based vocabulary list for food and drink in their vocabulary notebooks
2 practise translating and explaining a typical menu from their own language into English – either on their own or with a friend or colleague.

19 Living in Hong Kong

What did we do last time?

Do a review of the last type 1 lesson (Unit 16). Remind students of what they worked on (see Teacher's notes for that unit) and do some quick revision as follows.

The present continuous

Write these phrases on the board:
- now / at the moment
- current projects
- current changes and developments.

Remind them that they learnt that we use the present continuous to express these three different ideas. Can they give you sentences to illustrate each of these uses?

Ask them to convert some of the sentences into questions and negatives.

Sentence stress

Ask students to invent mini-dialogues to show how some words need extra stress. For example:

A: Can I borrow your car?
B: No, you can't! (disagreeing)

A: Do you work for Fiat?
B: No, I work for Renault. (correcting)

A: When will you see him?
B: I'll see him on Tuesday. (giving information in response to a *Wh-* question)

Encourage them to come up with similar ideas.

On the agenda: Why are we doing this?

Tell students the objectives of this lesson:
- to look at **should** and **have to**
- to talk about **organising a visit to another country**
- to do some pronunciation work on **stressing syllables in words**.

Reinforce this by writing the key words on the board or OHP.

Background briefing: Hong Kong

Hong Kong became a Special Administrative Region (SAR) of the People's Republic of China on July 1, 1997, after a century and a half of British administration. Under Hong Kong's constitutional document, the Basic Law, the existing economic, legal and social system will be maintained for 50 years. It has a population of nearly seven million and is a leading financial, trading and business centre with one of the world's best deep-water ports in the world. The official website says: 'A hardworking, adaptable and well-educated workforce of 3.42 million, coupled with entrepreneurial flair, is the bedrock of Hong Kong's productivity and creativity.' Situated at the south-eastern tip of China, and with a total area of 1,100 square kilometres, it covers Hong Kong Island, the Kowloon peninsula just opposite, and the New Territories – the more rural section of Hong Kong, which also includes 235 outlying islands. The population density is 6,250 people per square kilometre. The official languages are Chinese and English. The climate is sub-tropical. For more information, go to: www.info.gov.hk

(Tell students that Hong Kong promotional materials bill it as 'a world city'. You can also ask them now or later what a world city is and which other cities qualify.)

Warm up

- Look at the picture of John and read the caption.
- Look at the pictures of Hong Kong on the page and ask students to describe them.
- Ask them what they know about Hong Kong. You can ask about location, population, area, government, climate, etc.

Listen to this

Chinese culture

1
- Read the rubric and the four true/false statements. Ask students what they think the answers will be (unless you know that they are already very knowledgeable about Hong Kong).
- Check understanding of 'a tip' and 'to tip' before playing track 19.1.
- You may prefer the students to do exercise 2 as well before checking the answers to 1.

> **Answers**
> 1 F   2 T   3 T   4 F

2
- After playing track 19.1 again, ask students if they can reproduce some of the questions asked by the interviewer.
- Check their answers to one or both exercises, replaying selected passages from track 19.1 or checking on the tapescript if necessary.
- Ask students to find all the examples of 'should' and 'have to' in the tapescript of this interview.
- Can they formulate some rules for how to behave in Hong Kong, based on what John says (before you look at the next part of the lesson)?

> **Answers**
> 1 An older and more traditional Hong Kong and a younger, more westernised Hong Kong
> 2 Because modern houses and flats are so small
> 3 Ten or 15 per cent, or more if you're very happy with the service
> 4 Because people sometimes get into the train before other people have the chance to get out

Track 19.1 tapescript ▶▶

INTERVIEWER: Did you enjoy your time in Hong Kong?
JOHN: Yeah, it was a fantastic time. It's a very dynamic place.
INTERVIEWER: In business, when you meet people for the first time, can you use a first name quickly?
JOHN: Not really, it depends. The thing to say is that there are two Hong Kongs, a traditional Hong Kong with the older people and a young western Hong Kong. Young people move to first names quickly. With a traditional person, you have to use the surname to start with.
INTERVIEWER: And is it important to be on time in business?
JOHN: Yes, very important. Hong Kong is a very fast-moving place, people are always in a hurry and so yes, you really have to be on time if you want to do business.
INTERVIEWER: I have a friend who says it's typical to ask about salary, is that true?
JOHN: Yes, it's true, you can ask about salary. People are very open about money questions generally, and salary is a money question. So, don't be surprised if people ask you about that.
INTERVIEWER: And should you dress formally?
JOHN: Yes, formally to start with. Hong Kong is a very fashionable place, so you should dress well. You don't have to wear designer labels, but you should be smart.
INTERVIEWER: About general life, I think family is very important in Hong Kong culture?
JOHN: Yes, traditionally. In the past, families lived together, children, parents and grandparents. And there was a strong sense of family. Now, modern houses and flats are so small, families can't live together now, so things are changing.
INTERVIEWER: And are there any rules about tipping in taxis and restaurants, things like that?
JOHN: In Hong Kong tipping is very important. In restaurants you should tip, say ten per cent or 15 per cent, or more if you're very happy with the service.
INTERVIEWER: And finally, is there anything I should be careful about?
JOHN: Well, if you're in a train in the underground, and you want to get out, when the door opens, people often just push on before you can get out. It makes some tourists very angry. But the people are not rude, they simply want to do business quickly. You know, time is money in Hong Kong.

What do you think?

Ask students to identify the differences in terms of:
- first names for first meetings
- being on time for meetings
- asking people about their salaries
- how formally people dress
- the importance of family
- tipping
- pushing past in the subway/underground

Can they think of other possible areas of difference? Write these on the board.

Check your grammar

Should and *have to*

- Tell students that *should* can be used both to recommend and advise.
- Note *surname* here and in the interview with John Duncan. Point out that *surname* and *family name* are used interchangeably in English but be aware that this may cause confusion for some learners. For example, *surnom* in French means *nickname*.
- Ask them all to tell you something that:
  – we all have to do
  – we should do (recommendation)
  – we should do (advice).

> **Answers**
> 1 b   2 d   3 c   4 a

Do it yourself

> **Answers**
> **1** 1 You don't have to use surnames with the younger generation in Hong Kong.
> 2 You shouldn't disagree with your boss in a meeting.
> 3 Should I dress formally for the meeting? / Do I have to dress formally for the meeting?
> 4 He shouldn't smoke in here. People are trying to eat.
>
> **2** 1 have to   2 don't have to   3 should   4 has to
> 5 shouldn't

3 After playing track 19.2 to check the exercise, you can ask students to read the dialogue in pairs.

> **Answers**
> 1 b   2 f   3 d   4 a   5 c   6 e

Track 19.2 tapescript ▶▶

JAMES: Do you have to start work at the same time every day?
COLLEAGUE: No. You can choose any time between 7.30 and 9.30.
JAMES: Do you have to work 40 hours every week?

COLLEAGUE:	Yes, you have to work the hours in your contract.
JAMES:	Do you have to wear a tie at work?
COLLEAGUE:	You don't have to unless you are meeting a customer.
JAMES:	Should I buy my boss a present? It's her birthday tomorrow.
COLLEAGUE:	Yes, you should, but just something simple and not too expensive.
JAMES:	Should I inform Peter about the computer problem?
COLLEAGUE:	Yes, I think you should. He wants to know about any IT questions.
JAMES:	Should I send him an email to confirm the meeting?
COLLEAGUE:	No, you don't have to. I've already told him the time and place.

Sounds good

Word stress

Note: We hope that students will always have access to a good learner's dictionary like the *Cambridge Learner's Dictionary* during lessons, but please note that dictionaries are particularly useful for the pronunciation part of this lesson.

1. - Ask selected students to pronounce the two words 'China' and 'Chinese' and ask where the main stress falls in each word. Then play track 19.3 to confirm or correct their efforts. Do the same with 'Japan' and 'Japanese'.
   - Read the rubric and ask students to provide one or two of their own examples of words with two or more syllables. Ask them each time which syllable has the main stress.
   - Suggest ways that they can mark this: by highlighting, underlining, circling, etc. or, when writing, writing the stressed syllable in capital letters.

2. Play track 19.4 and ask students to identify the stressed syllables. Then get them to repeat each phrase as they give you their answers.

Answers
1 fan<u>tas</u>tic   2 dy<u>nam</u>ic   3 tra<u>di</u>tional   4 <u>mon</u>ey
5 <u>fash</u>ionable   6 im<u>por</u>tant   7 <u>mod</u>ern   8 per <u>cent</u>

Tracks 19.3 and 19.4 tapescripts ▶▶
See Student's Book.

Pronunciation quiz
- If students have access to a dictionary like the *Cambridge Learner's Dictionary*, show them how stressed syllables are accented within the phonetic transcription and explain that they don't even have to be able to read the phonetics to check this. When they listen to the pronunciation of a word on the dictionary's CD ROM or elsewhere, they should always note where the stress falls in an unfamiliar word.
- Give students time to prepare their list of words and to check pronunciation – with you if necessary.
- Have them do the quiz in pairs while you go round checking.
- Take selected words from the students' lists and try them out on the whole class.

It's time to talk

Explain the situation, which involves asking for recommendations and cultural guidance. Check how students form statements, negatives and questions using *should* and *have to*. Then proceed as usual for a pairwork activity with file cards. Notice that Bs do not have to ask questions, so reversing roles might be helpful after students have done the activity once.

What did we do today?
Check the Remember section quickly and remind students of the objectives of this lesson.

Follow up
Encourage students to:
1 write six sentences to recommend or advise using *should*
2 write six sentences about rules using *have to*
3 write other sentences about cultural differences between the student's own culture and another. (For example: In my country/organisation/family, we do X. In country/organisation/family Y, they do Z.)
4 decide how best they like to mark the stress on the stressed syllable in words with two or more syllables
5 mark the main stress on words with more than one syllable in their vocabulary books and practise pronouncing them.

20 Online

What did we do last time?
Do a review of the last type 2 lesson (Unit 17). Remind students of what they worked on (see Teacher's notes for that unit) and do some quick revision as follows.

Communication verbs
How many communication verbs can students think of? We hope they will remember:
speak talk ask explain listen call discuss write reply call interrupt

Write their suggestions on the board and ask them to make sentences with the words they have suggested. Pay special attention to their use of prepositions with verbs like 'listen' and 'explain'.

Replying to emails
Ask students what they might write in reply to an email at these stages in their reply:
- to greet
- to begin politely
- to close.

Give them these examples of the main bodies of emails they could receive and ask them to write one-sentence action points in reply:
- Can we meet at 11.30 next Wednesday?

- Please would you send me some information about your services?
- Is it possible to have a 10% discount on the price we usually pay?

On the agenda: Why are we doing this?
Tell students the objectives of this lesson:
- to talk about **people and their computers**
- to learn **computer vocabulary**
- to practise **arranging meetings by phone** (to arrange a meeting is the same as to fix a meeting).

Reinforce this by writing the key words on the board or OHP.

Warm up

Ask students the questions and write answers on the board. Give help with vocabulary where necessary. You should get some of these:
- word processing
- surfing the Internet for fun
- online shopping
- sending and receiving emails
- online chatting
- homework/study
- personal finance
- games
- travel information
- booking tickets
- getting information for your job, etc.

How many students have a computer at home and at work?

Then look at the picture of Mike Parker and read the caption.

Read on

Computer heaven or hell?

1
- Read the rubric and the four headings and check understanding of *website* and *online*.
- Get students to do the matching as a skimming exercise. After the exercise, ask them how they proceeded: which key words did they spot in the text which helped them to do the task? (e.g. *problems* in line 2 of paragraph A, *shopping* in line 2 of paragraph B, *Spanish* in line 5 of paragraph C, and *website designer* in line 2 of paragraph D.)

Answers
1 D   2 B   3 A   4 C

2
- Read the four questions and ask selected students to read the paragraphs aloud round the class.
- After each of the four paragraphs has been read, ask students if they have the answer to any of the questions.
- When you have the four answers, ask each student to write one more comprehension question to ask the others. Work through these questions as well, checking for grammatical accuracy.
- Ask students to go through the text to identify all the computer-related words. Check understanding of all of these.

Answers
1 Over 50.
2 They hate shopping in real shops and it's easy to use.
3 Schoolwork, chatting to friends and learning Spanish.
4 Over 12 hours.

What do you think?

Ask the question and elicit answers. How much time do students spend in front of a computer – at work and at home? Is this more or less than the time they spend watching TV? Would they like to spend more or less time in front of a computer? What is the ideal amount of time per day or per week?

The words you need ... to talk about computers and the Internet

1 Students who are familiar with computer vocabulary will find this exercise quite easy but others may find it difficult. Be prepared to do some pre-teaching by asking the following questions:
- What do you do to your computer when you arrive in your office in the morning? (*switch on*)
- Do you have to enter a special word? What do we call it? What are you doing? (*password/logging on*)
- If you want to type a report or a letter, what is the first thing you do? (*create a document/file*)
- What do you do to get a paper copy? (*print*) etc.

Then ask them: What computer problems do you have at work? Don't allow this discussion to go on for too long!

Answers
1 log on   2 created   3 saved   4 print   5 resend
1 c   2 a   3 b

2 After the exercise, talk about rules for using the Internet. How many of them have access to the Internet at work? (In some countries and organisations, access at work is very restricted.)

Answers
1 connect   2 online   3 intranet   4 surf   5 virus   6 chat

It's time to talk

Students can use the statements in the book and their own sentences to build a picture of their partner's computing habits. Do a class survey during the debriefing to get an overall picture of the computing behaviour of the group. Ask students for the addresses of their favourite websites to share with the others. Remind them that regular surfing is a great way to learn English because of the opportunities to read and because of all the materials for learning which are available today, not least at the Cambridge University Press site: www.cambridge/org/elt

COMMUNICATING AT WORK
Telephoning 3: Arranging meetings by phone

Start by doing some quick revision of the work you did on telephoning in Unit 2 on getting information by phone. Ask them for phrases you can use:
- to answer a call
- to say who is calling and to ask for someone
- to give a reason for your call
- to finish a call.

1

> **Answers**
>
> Philippe – Friday – 14.00
> Frank – Monday – 13.00
> Petra – Tuesday – 10.00

2

> **Answers**
>
> Is it possible to have a meeting?
> When are you free?
> See you next week.
> I'm calling to fix a meeting.
> I'm sorry, I can't.
> See you on Tuesday at 10.

3

Finish this section by asking students to identify and review the new language which they should try to learn.

Track 20.1 Tapescript ▶▶

Philippe

PHILIPPE: Jim, is it possible to have a meeting next week? I'd like to discuss some technical problems with our computer network.
JIM: Sure, Philippe, no problem. When are you free?
PHILIPPE: What about next Friday at two o'clock, after lunch?
JIM: Fine. Can you send me an email to confirm that?
PHILIPPE: OK. See you next week. Bye.

Frank

FRANK: Jim, it's Frank. I'm calling to fix a meeting next week to discuss the Bolivia project. When are you free?
JIM: What about Monday at 12 o'clock?
FRANK: I'm sorry, I can't. I have another meeting. What about 1 o'clock?
JIM: OK, 1 on Monday.
FRANK: Thanks, Jim. Bye.

Petra

PETRA: Jim, it's Petra. How are you?
JIM: I'm fine. How are you?
PETRA: Fine. I'm calling because I'm in town next week. Are you free at all?
JIM: Sure. When?
PETRA: For me, Tuesday would be best … at ten o'clock?
JIM: Just a moment … yes, that's fine. See you on Tuesday at 10.
PETRA: Great. And I have those pictures from the conference for you.
JIM: Really? Great. See you next week, Petra. Take care. Bye.

What did we do today?
Check the Remember section quickly and remind students of the objectives of this lesson.

Follow up
Encourage students to:
1 write sentences about computer use and computer procedures
2 do a survey of students' or colleagues' computing habits (based on the ideas in It's time to talk) and write up the results in a short report.

21 Beirut Intercontinental

What did we do last time?
Do a review of the last type 3 lesson (Unit 18). Remind students of what they worked on (see Teacher's notes for that unit) and do some quick revision as follows.

At the restaurant
Ask students to brainstorm phrases for different stages involved in going out for a meal: arriving, ordering the starter and main course, checking that everything is OK during the meal, ordering dessert, and paying. You could also ask them to act out different stages in the process, with one waiter or waitress to two or three guests.

Food and drink
Ask students what the difference is between: *cuisine*, *cook* and *cooker*; *dessert* and *desert*; *plate* and *dish*.
Ask for five (or more?) different types of meat, fish (usually the hardest), vegetable, fruit and drink.

On the agenda: Why are we doing this?
Tell students the objectives of this lesson:
- to practise useful phrases for **staying in a hotel**
- to learn and practise useful **hotels and hotel service** vocabulary.

Reinforce this by writing the key words on the board or OHP.

Warm up
- Ask the question. Find out which are the most important things for the group.
- Ask students to tell you what they can see in the backdrop photo. Where is it? Would they like to stay there? Why? Why not?

Enjoy your stay

> **Answers**
>
> 1 g   2 h   3 e   4 f   5 b   6 i   7 j   8 d   9 c   10 a

Unit twenty-one 59

Track 21.1 tapescript ▶▶

Checking in

A: Hello, my name's Sanchez, I have a reservation.
B: Good evening. Yes, Mr Sanchez, a single room, for two nights. Could you complete this form, please?
A: Of course.
B: Thank you. So, it's room 414, on the fourth floor. Do you need any help with your bags?
A: No, thanks. I can manage.

A morning call

A: Hello, can I have breakfast in my room, please? At 7 o'clock?
B: Certainly, sir.
A: So I'd like a wake-up call at 6.30. Can you do that?
B: That's fine. So, morning call at 6.30, breakfast at 7 o'clock.

A problem

A: Good morning. There's a problem with the shower. There's no hot water. Can you send someone to look at it?
B: Of course, I'll send someone immediately. What's your room number?
A: 414.
B: Fine. Someone will be with you in a moment.

Leaving

A: Morning, can I check out, please? Room 414.
B: Right, Mr Sanchez. Anything from the minibar last night?
A: No, nothing.
B: OK, here's your bill. Sign here, please. Have a good trip home.

Have a go

Can students role-play other hotel situations?

Listen to this

It's a great place to stay

Look at the picture of Bob Hands and read the caption:
- How many nights a year do students spend in hotels? On business? For pleasure?
- Would they like to spend 200 nights a year (nearly four nights a week) in hotels like Bob?

1 Ask students to describe the three pictures before doing the exercise.

> **Answers**
> Hotel 3

2 After the exercise, ask students to summarise what Bob likes about this hotel.

> **Answers**
> 1 F   2 F   3 T   4 F

Track 21.2 tapescript ▶▶

BOB: So, where is my favourite hotel? It's difficult but I think my favourite, favourite hotel is Le Vendôme Intercontinental in Beirut. It's only a four-star hotel because it doesn't have a swimming pool but for me it's perfect. It's small – it only has about 70 rooms so it's very cosy. The staff are very friendly, they always remember my name, even the chambermaids. I like good food, and Le Vendôme has a first-class French restaurant. I love French food, you know! And ... oh yes, just outside the door there is a very, very nice fountain which I like, in the Spanish style. I stay there quite a lot and for me it's like going home to see friends. They meet you at the airport, take you straight to your room, there are no forms to fill in ... you feel very, very comfortable. And one more thing, on the roof there is a really famous bar called Sidney's where they serve the breakfasts in the morning. It has a beautiful view over the Mediterranean with the fishing boats ... mmm, I think I can smell the coffee and the sea ...

What do you think?

Ask students about their favourite hotels: names, locations, what makes them special, what makes a good hotel, plus horror stories – in brief, what is their worst hotel experience?

The words you need ... for staying in hotels

1 Ask students to do the exercise and then to make up their own sentences, each using a word in the box.

> **Answers**
> 1 key   2 cancel   3 recommend   4 double room
> 5 towels   6 change   7 corridor   8 connect

2 Students can match the pictures with the problems on their own. Then ask them to role-play dialogues between receptionist and guests with problems. They can do all five situations and then reverse roles.

> **Answers**
> 1 b   2 a   3 e   4 d   5 c

It's time to talk

Players can use coins to move with. If you are asked to rule, decide whether the phrase would be comprehensible to the receptionist, i.e. use fluency rather than accuracy as your main criterion – unless you want to be really strict!

What did we do today?

Check the Remember section quickly and remind students of the objectives of this lesson.

Follow up

Encourage students to write down their own list of phrases which could be useful in hotels.

22 Working for Rolls Royce

What did we do last time?
Do a review of the last type 1 lesson (Unit 19). Remind students of what they worked on (see Teacher's notes for that unit) and do some quick revision as follows.

Should and *have to*
Ask students to give you some tips for people coming to live and work in their country or countries, for example:
- Women should not wear trousers in the office.
- Men should always wear a tie.
- You have to be on time for meetings.

Word stress
Write these words on the board:

important   fantastic   traditional   dynamic   fashionable

For each one, ask students to:
- tell you how many syllables there are
- tell you which is the stressed syllable
- pronounce the word for you.

Can students suggest their own words with three syllables or more?

On the agenda: Why are we doing this?
Tell students the objectives of this lesson:
- to look at **many**, **much**, **a few** and **a little**
- to talk about **numbers and quantity**
- to **practise saying numbers**.

Reinforce this by writing the key words on the board or OHP.

Warm up
- Ask the two warm-up questions. Do they take work home with them at night? Do they work at weekends?
- Look at the picture of Isabelle and read the caption.
- Look at the pictures taken at Rolls Royce and ask the students to describe them. What kind of company is it? What does it do?

Background briefing
Rolls Royce is actually two quite different companies. Rolls Royce Group is an engineering company in the aerospace, defence and marine industries (www.rolls-royce.com), perhaps best known for its aero engines. The luxury cars are made by Rolls Royce Motor Cars Ltd, now a subsidiary of BMW (www.rolls-roycemotorcars.com). Isabelle's company in France is part of the former.

Listen to this

Work is like a second home

> **Answers**
> 1 Number of employees: 4
>   Meetings per week: 2–3
>   Working hours per week: 35
>   Holiday weeks per year: 6

2 Check students' answers and ask them to give corresponding answers about themselves. Alternatively, you could play or read from the tapescript selected sentences from Isabelle's answers and ask students to make similar statements, for example:
- I have a lot of emails to write and read, so this takes maybe around 75–80% of my time.
- I start at 9, have one hour for lunch and finish at 5.15.
- Holidays? . . . I normally take three weeks in August.

Ask:
- how many meetings students attend each week
- how many of them are important or useful
- how many they would like to attend.

> **Answers**
> 1 She makes herself a big cup of coffee.
> 2 75–80% of her time
> 3 She has six weeks' holiday, but no other benefits.
> 4 She likes working for a British company; she speaks English a lot; she feels part of a team.

Track 22.1 tapescript ▶▶

INTERVIEWER: So, Isabelle, how many people work for Rolls Royce?

ISABELLE: Well, Rolls Royce Group is a big company but our office in France is a small representative office with only four people: two directors, one engineer and myself.

INTERVIEWER: So what is a typical day? How much time do you spend on the telephone and with email?

ISABELLE: Well, first of all I make myself a big cup of coffee. That is very important. Then the telephone. OK, it's not too bad but I have a lot of emails to write and read, so this takes maybe around 75 to 80% of my time.

INTERVIEWER: What about meetings? Do you go to many meetings?

ISABELLE: No, I don't, no. In France, a lot of people spend too much time in meetings, but I'm lucky. I have to go to a few, maybe two a week, but not too many.

INTERVIEWER: And how many hours per week do you work?

ISABELLE: Well, as you know, in France we have a 35-hour working week now, so I start work at nine, have one hour for lunch and finish at five-fifteen. Of course, the directors work a lot more, sometimes at weekends. But for me, the 35-hour working week is good. I even leave at four-thirty on Fridays sometimes.

INTERVIEWER: What about benefits and holidays?

ISABELLE: Well, that one is easy, no benefits at all. I mean, no mobile phone, or company car, no, not for me. It's a pity! Holidays? Well, it's now six weeks and I normally take three weeks in August, which is typical in France.

INTERVIEWER: And, one final question, do you like your job?

ISABELLE: I do like my job, yes, because … well, I like working for a

British company. I speak and work in English all day and that's really very nice for me, I like that. I also feel like a member of the team rather than just a secretary. And, generally, working here, it's like a second home. It's a real pleasure to come here every day.

Check your grammar

Many, much, a few, a little

- Check that students remember what they learnt about countable and uncountable nouns in Unit 7. Can they give several examples of both types?
- You could also ask students to work in pairs to make their own sentences illustrating each of the quantifiers (*many*, *much*, *a few* and *a little*).

Answers

1 a few   2 much   3 many   4 a little

Do it yourself

Answers

1   1 I don't give many presentations in my job.
    2 Do you want a little milk with your coffee?
    3 How much information do you have about our new product?
    4 I'm sorry but I need a little more time to write this report.

2   1 many   2 much   3 many   4 much   5 many   6 many
    7 much   8 many

3   1 a lot of / a few   2 much / a lot of   3 a little
    4 a few   5 many

4   Students could ask and answer questions about the information they give in pairs.

Sounds good

Saying numbers and prices

You could warm up with a simple number test for the whole class, for example by asking students to write down a series of numbers like: 37, 450, 983, 1, 100, 3, 650, etc. Then get them to read them back to you and write what they give you on the board. They should note in particular how the 'and' follows hundreds in British English as in 'four hundred and fifty'.

Answers and Track 22.2 tapescript ▶▶

Numbers
25	twenty-five
100	a hundred *or* one hundred
101	a hundred and one *or* one hundred and one
1,000	a thousand *or* one thousand
2,001	two thousand and one
10,550	ten thousand five hundred and fifty
500,000	five hundred thousand
1,000,000	a million *or* one million
1,000,000,000	a billion *or* one billion

Prices
50p	fifty p
£4.99	four pounds ninety-nine p *or* four pounds ninety-nine
£250	two hundred and fifty pounds
€150,000	a hundred and fifty thousand euros *or* one hundred and fifty thousand euros
£150m	a hundred and fifty million pounds *or* one hundred and fifty million pounds
$0.99	ninety-nine cents
$4.95	four dollars ninety-five cents *or* four dollars ninety-five
$2,500	two thousand five hundred dollars
$2.5m	two point five million dollars *or* two and a half million dollars

It's time to talk

Introduce the activity by saying that it is designed to give students the chance to practise using numbers and quantities in a realistic situation. Student A is going to call Student B to get some information, so the basic objective is simply to communicate the numbers successfully. You can check this by asking the As for the information they have noted.

But ask them too, as they work, to think about the quantities involved: isn't 23 sales people rather a lot? Student As may also wish to comment on the figures they hear and Bs could try to justify them.

What did we do today?

Check the Remember section quickly and remind students of the objectives of this lesson.

Follow up

Encourage students to write down sentences about the news in the week to come or about their organisations containing:
- numbers and prices
- *many*, *much*, *a few* and *a little*

which they can also practise saying aloud.

23 Start up

What did we do last time?

Do a review of the last type 2 lesson (Unit 20). Remind students of what they worked on (see Teacher's notes for that unit) and do some quick revision as follows.

Computer vocabulary

Ask students to give you sentences describing some routine computer processes and procedures. If necessary, ask prompting questions like: *What's the first thing you do with your computer when you get to work in the morning? Then what?* etc. Aim to elicit words like: *save, delete, website, intranet, laptop, attached file, virus, password*, etc.

Arranging meetings by phone
Ask students to give you phrases to:
- open a call
- give the reason for your call (to fix a meeting)
- suggest a date, time and place
- suggest an alternative date, time and place
- confirm
- close

Ask one or two pairs of selected students to perform spontaneous dialogues before the class.

On the agenda: Why are we doing this?
Tell students the objectives of this lesson:
- to talk about **solving a business problem**
- to learn **money and business finance** vocabulary
- to practise **helping visitors**.

Reinforce this by writing the key words on the board or OHP.

Warm up
- Ask students the three questions. You could ask them to rate difficulty on a scale of 1 to 5. Do any of them have / have any of them ever had a small business?
- Look at the photos and read the caption. Ask students to describe what they see. What do they think they could buy in the Tower Street Pantry?

Read on

Managing a small business
1. - Read the rubric and the five questions.
   - Ask the students: If you did an interview with Jackie Black, which order would you ask these questions in?
   - Ask the students to quickly skim the text in order to do the matching. As in previous units, ask them what key words helped them to do the task.
   - Check their answers. If there is disagreement, wait until they've read the paragraphs again before commenting.

Answers
1 D   2 E   3 B   4 A   5 C

2. - Can students invent their own comprehension questions?
   - How many words relating to money and finance can they find in the text? Do they understand them all?

Answers
1 Four years ago
2 A member of their family lent them the money.
3 Fresh fruit and vegetables
4 Profits doubled (they increased by 100%).
5 Because they can make more money this way: the margins are higher

What do you think?
Ask students if they agree with Jackie and Phil's approach to running a food business.

The words you need ... to talk about money and business finance

1. You can also ask students to make general sentences from the words in the boxes of both exercises 1 and 2 to show understanding of their meanings.

Answers
1 turnover   2 profit   3 costs   4 margin   5 budget

2. Ask them to make sentences using the same verbs again, if possible about their organisation.

Answers
1 make   2 borrow   3 increase   4 invest   5 pay

It's time to talk
- Try to keep the language of each meeting as simple as possible.
- The main difficulty for the group may be deciding on a procedure. You may wish higher level students to work one out for themselves (which could take some time but which is in itself valuable language and communication skills practice). For other groups, you can suggest that they start by making their individual choices, then comparing notes and eliminating options not favoured by anyone.
- With bigger groups, you can turn this into a pyramid exercise, where first of all individuals decide on their strategy, then you put them into pairs who have to compromise on a joint strategy, then put two pairs to agree, etc. Keep a strict time limit on each stage. Ask the whole group finally to present the class solution to you.

COMMUNICATING AT WORK

Helping visitors

In this part, students will work on what to do and say to help visitors with problems.
Start by asking students what kind of problems visitors can have. For example:
- a lost suitcase
- lost money and/or documents
- no money
- can't remember the name or location of their hotel
- need to find a special kind of shop, etc.

and ask them their general answer to the introductory question.

1

Answers
1 b   2 c   3 d   4 a

2. You could ask students to repeat the gist of each dialogue in mini role-plays.

Unit twenty-three 63

Answers

Follow me.
Do you want to borrow some money?I
Would you like to use a computer here?
I can show you on the map if you want.

Track 23.1 tapescript ▶▶|

1
A: Excuse me, I think I'm lost. Can you tell me where Room 101 is?
B: I can show you.
A: Really? That's very kind of you.
B: No problem. Follow me.

2
A: Your bill.
B: Thank you. Oh no. Caroline?
C: What is it?
B: I don't have any money. I'm really sorry.
C: Do you want to borrow some money?
B: Can I? Twenty euros? I'll pay you back tomorrow.
C: No problem. Here you are.
B: Thanks.

3
A: Excuse me. I need to send an email. Can I plug in my computer?
B: Would you like to use a computer here?
A: Yes, thanks.
B: The computer in the corner is free.
A: Thank you for your help.

4
A: Sandra, could you recommend a restaurant for me tonight?
B: Sure. There's an excellent Chinese place I know.
A: Great. Where is it?
B: I can show you on the map, if you want.
A: Yes, thanks.

3 Read through How to take care of a visitor and ask students to role-play the dialogues in pairs. Can they add a situation of their own for the others to identify?

What did we do today?
Check the Remember section quickly and remind students of the objectives of this lesson.

Follow up
Encourage students to:
1 write sentences about personal finance and the finance of the organisation they work for
2 listen, look for and write down sentences about finance in the news which contain money and finance terms in this unit.

24 I buy money

What did we do last time?
Do a review of the last type 3 lesson (Unit 21). Remind students of what they worked on (see Teacher's notes for that unit) and do some quick revision as follows.

Staying in a hotel
Ask students to make useful sentences for hotels by completing these phrases:
- Could you . . . ?
- Do you need . . . ?
- Can I have . . . ?
- There's a problem . . .
- I'll send . . .
- There's no . . .

Which of these is likely to be spoken by a guest, which by a member of a hotel's staff, and which by either?

Hotels and hotel service
Ask students to tell a short story (one sentence per key word) about a hotel, using these groups of words. They may like to have them written on the board:
- reservation – double room – twin room – bill
- key – corridor – towel – reception
- floor – lift – bag – tip
- room service – wake-up call – breakfast – check out

You can offer your own suggestions. For example:
- I heard a noise in the corridor outside my room.
- I went out of my room in just a towel to see what it was.
- The door closed behind me and I didn't have my key.
- I had to go down to reception to ask for another key to get back in!

On the agenda: Why are we doing this?
Tell students the objectives of this lesson:
- to practise useful phrases for **talking about money**
- to learn and practise useful **money and shopping vocabulary**.

Reinforce this by writing the key words on the board or OHP.

Warm up
- Ask the questions. Does anyone prefer saving to spending?
- Ask the students to describe what they see in the backdrop photo. Is this the perfect place for an afternoon out or the kind of place they never visit?

Money talk

Answers
1 i   2 d   3 e   4 g   5 c   6 j   7 a   8 h   9 f   10 b

Track 24.1 tapescript ⏭

Asking a colleague for money
A: Clare, I haven't got much cash on me.
B: Do you want to borrow some money?
A: Could you lend me ten pounds until tomorrow?
B: No problem.
A: Cheers. That's very nice of you.

Getting money out
A: Shall we find a restaurant?
B: Yes, but I need to get some money out first.
A: OK, I'll wait here.
B: Is there a cash point nearby?
A: Yes, there's a bank just across the road, over there.

Changing money
A: Hello, I'd like to change some euros into Swiss francs.
B: How much do you want to change?
A: What's the commission?
B: There's no commission if you change more than 200 euros.
A: OK, then I'll change 300, thanks.

Getting change
A: Excuse me, do you have any change?
B: What do you need?
A: I need some coins for the coffee machine.
B: Just a second, yes, here you are.
A: Thanks very much.

Have a go

Can students role-play other situations involving money?

Listen to this

Hey, big spender

(The heading is the title of what is perhaps big-voiced Dame Shirley Bassey's best-known song. There is an unconfirmed story that officials at Liverpool Airport have played a recording of this at high volume to move pigeons from the runway.)

Look at the pictures of Anne, Tashi and Sam. Explain that they are going to hear how these people like to spend their money.

1 What do your students find it hard to resist buying? Books? Chocolate? Clothes? Students with a visual imagination might like to draw a picture of themselves similar to the three illustrations in the book.

> **Answers**
> **1** 1 b   2 c   3 a
>
> **2** 1 On Saturday mornings
>   2 For holidays
>   3 Old coins
>   4 No. He spends without thinking.
>   5 Belgian chocolate
>   6 Almost every month

Track 24.2 tapescript ⏭

1
INTERVIEWER: Anne, what do you spend your money on?
ANNE: I like shopping for clothes. That's my usual Saturday morning activity. But I don't spend a lot. I look for reasonable prices.
INTERVIEWER: OK, and anything else?
ANNE: Not really. I save money every year so that I can have a good holiday. This year it's China. Oh, and one final thing, of course, about money. I have five cats and so I spend a lot of money on cat food.

2
INTERVIEWER: What kind of things do you spend money on?
TASHI: Well, I have an unusual hobby, I'm very interested in old coins. You could say, I buy money. And I really like unusual ones so I have some from China, Tibet and Bhutan, for example, and some interesting ones from Greece too. I ask people I meet about coins and if I see something very unusual on the street I buy it, and when I travel I also try and get some for my collection.
INTERVIEWER: Do you like spending money?
TASHI: Actually no, I don't, but I do spend it! I think I should be saving but I keep spending. I don't know where I spend it, it just goes. If I see some coins I buy them and if I see some nice clothes I buy them, I mean without thinking about whether I have the money or not!

3
INTERVIEWER: So, Sam, what do you spend your money on at the weekend?
SAM: Everything. I'm terrible. I'm really bad with money. My purse is always empty! But every Saturday morning I always buy Belgian chocolate for my friends and then we have a coffee together in the city. I'm very generous with chocolate!
INTERVIEWER: Sounds nice. Do you buy anything special?
SAM: Shoes! I love shoes. I buy new shoes almost every month.
INTERVIEWER: Every month? What does your husband say?
SAM: Oh, he's a dangerous shopper too!

What do you think?

How do students manage their money?

The words you need ... to talk about money

1 Do students agree with these rules? Ask them to work in pairs to find out from each other what they spend their money on and which of the rules they follow.

> **Answers**
> 1 on   2 in   3 for   4 by   5 for   6 with

2
- Ask students to do the exercise and also to add their own words and phrases to each box.
- Organising vocabulary by topic is one good way to learn new words. Can students think of other useful topic areas for learning vocabulary? Do they have other techniques? (See also Better learning activities 10 on pages 115 and 125.)

Unit twenty-four

> **Answers**
> 1 generous   2 notes   3 get   4 reasonable

It's time to talk

- Students should first decide individually how they would spend the money. Then ask them to interview each other in pairs.
- Students should then check partners' scores and report back to the class. Do they have other ideas about how to spend a large sum of money?

What did we do today?
Check the Remember section quickly and remind students of the objectives of this lesson.

Follow up
Encourage students to:
1 write down words and phrases about money which they recognise from a financial newspaper
2 write their own sentences using money vocabulary introduced in this unit.

25 Driving to Romania

What did we do last time?
Do a review of the last type 1 lesson (Unit 22). Remind students of what they worked on (see Teacher's notes for that unit) and do some quick revision as follows.

Numbers and quantity: many, much, a few and a little
Ask students (and write on the board if necessary):
- How many hours a week do you work?
- How much time do you spend on emails?

Now ask them why one question uses *much* and the other uses *many*.
Can they give you some countable and uncountable nouns and make questions or sentences with them using *many, much, a few* and *a little*?

Saying numbers
Do a quick number dictation to the class or write on the board for them to say, as follows:
1   123
2   123,456,789
3   00 33 1 42 64 96 89
4   €25.90
5   £300m

On the agenda: Why are we doing this?
Tell students the objectives of this lesson:
- to look at how we can use the **present continuous for future plans**
- to do more **pronunciation** work on **weak stress**.

Reinforce this by writing the key words on the board or OHP.

Warm up
Explain that you are going to talk about people's future plans and give students one or two examples of your plans using the present continuous, for example:
- I'm meeting some friends tonight.
- I'm playing football / having a party at the weekend.

After this:
- Ask them to ask each other the two questions in the Warm up in pairs and get some quick third person feedback on the answers.
- Look at the photo of Anthony Allen. Ask them to describe what they can see. Then read the caption and check comprehension, especially *orphan*.
- Explain that they are going to hear about Anthony and learn about his future plans.

Background briefing
Selsey is a small town on the south coast of England where this children's charity was started in 1991 in response to the terrible conditions which the world began to understand were being experienced by thousands of children in Romanian orphanages. Its first projects involved the delivery of three articulated lorries full of aid collected in Selsey and the surrounding area. SROA also teamed up with another group from Britain to refurbish a sanatorium that was more of a hazard to health than a help for the children that were in there. They successfully refurbished the building and were able to dramatically improve the conditions for the children. During the next two years they continued to deliver lorries of aid to orphanages and institutions. It became a registered British charity in 1993.

Since then they have also focused on helping to slow down the flow of babies into the orphanages by helping medical dispensaries, schools and kindergartens, particularly in outlying rural areas.

Their main work, however, continues to involve building, refurbishing, digging wells and septic tanks, plumbing, electrics and sanitation and they still continue to supply medical equipment and medical supplies, toys, shoes and general supplies to orphanages, medical dispensaries and schools. All their projects are ongoing and they generally visit them all at least twice a year to carry out maintenance on all previous work and to begin new work. All their workers are volunteers and receive no remuneration. For more information, go to: sroauk.org.uk

Listen to this

A job everyone wants to do

1 Look at the picture of a children's home in Romania and ask students to describe what they can see before doing the exercise.

> **Answers**
> 1 F   2 F   3 T   4 F

66 Teacher's notes: Units 1–30

2
- After playing track 25.1 again to check the answers, ask if students can remember any of the interviewer's questions (or Anthony's answers). Offer prompts like *How . . . ?* and *How long . . . ?*
- You could also listen to the track again or look at the tapescript to focus on how the interviewer and Anthony use the present continuous to talk about his future plans.

> **Answers**
> 1 He saw a lot of television programmes about Romanian children's homes and wanted to help.
> 2 To make the children's homes a better place to live
> 3 To build a hospital
> 4 Nothing – they are volunteers

Track 25.1 tapescript ▶▶

INTERVIEWER: So, Anthony, tell me a little about your organisation and what you do.

ANTHONY: I work for a local hospital. And in the Selsey Romania Orphans Appeal, I'm the chairman, and main coordinator, so everything, really. I started the Selsey Romania Orphans Appeal in 1991, I think it was.

INTERVIEWER: And why did you start the charity?

ANTHONY: I saw a lot of television programmes about Romanian children's homes with babies in a terrible, terrible situation, and I had to help. So we organised people to go out there, and now we have around 28 people all in all who support our work, and I think we make a difference to the quality of life for these children.

INTERVIEWER: What do you do out in Romania?

ANTHONY: Well, our first and main objective was to make the children's homes a better place to live. When we arrived, they were terrible: no fresh water, no modern toilet system, no clean kitchens, you can't imagine. There was so much to do to make things like a normal place to live.

INTERVIEWER: You've done a lot of work already. Is there still a lot to do in the future?

ANTHONY: Oh, yes. Absolutely. Eight of us, I think, no nine, are travelling there later this year in October to start a new project.

INTERVIEWER: And how are you getting there?

ANTHONY: Well, we're not flying, we're driving, believe it or not! We have an old bus and we normally hire a van to take out all the usual things like clothes and toys and even building materials.

INTERVIEWER: How long are you staying?

ANTHONY: We're staying for two weeks. Two weeks is the normal period. And this time we want to install new washing machines and also take some medical equipment. Then the big, big project next year is to build a hospital.

INTERVIEWER: Wow, this sounds like a big job. Is it hard work?

ANTHONY: Not at all. We go because we want to go, because we want to help. No one gets any money or salary in the charity, not one pound, dollar or euro. We're all volunteers. This is one job that everyone is very, very happy to do.

INTERVIEWER: Where do you get the finance for your projects?

ANTHONY: People give us money. We get nothing from the government – just ordinary people, people want to help too and the best way they can do that is to give money to us so that we can give the help directly to the children.

INTERVIEWER: Thanks, Anthony. Good luck with all your projects.

ANTHONY: Thank you very much.

What do you think?

First check understanding of 'charity'. Then ask if students would like to do some other charity work abroad – for example, after they retire or by taking a year out? Where would they go? What would they do?

Check your grammar

The present continuous 2

> **Answers**
> 1 doing   2 are / 're   3 Are   4 am   5 aren't / 're not

Do it yourself

1

> **Answers**
> 1 I'm giving a presentation next week.
> 2 Is your boss coming to the meeting?
> 3 Are you going to the theatre tonight?
> 4 I'm not coming to the theatre tonight. I'm tired.

2 Read the rubric and allow students a little time to look through the conversation between Anthony and Anna. Check comprehension of words like *architect* and *government official*.

> **Answers**
> 1 we're not meeting / we aren't meeting
> 2 We're seeing
> 3 when are you going
> 4 we're running
> 5 Are you still coming
> 6 we're having

Track 25.2 tapescript ▶▶

ANTHONY: Anna, it's Anthony. I just wanted to discuss the hospital schedule and check you agree with everything.

ANNA: Sure. Go ahead.

ANTHONY: OK, we're not meeting the architects in October. We're seeing them in November instead.

ANNA: Right. So when are you going to Bucharest for the meeting with the government officials?

ANTHONY: On 18th December. And just before that, on December 14th, we're running a seminar to inform everyone in SROA about the project. Are you still coming to England next year?

ANNA: Yes, in January.

ANTHONY: Good. Well, we're having a tour of my local hospital at the end of January to meet some doctors who are part of the project. I think that's everything.

ANNA: Good. See you soon.

3
- Read the rubric and the email from Kim and ask the students to consult the notes before writing their replies. You might want to provide a first sentence (see Answer on following page) that they can use as a model for the rest.
- Go round checking their efforts at the same time as they check each other's. Tell students that the time

limit for this activity is 5 to 7 minutes and stick to it. Don't let them spend too much time writing.
- Provide feedback to the class both on problem areas and to cite examples of good writing.

Model answer

From:
To: Kim Copeland
Subject: Workshop

Dear Kim
Thank you for your email. Regarding the workshop:
1 Participants
   Anna Parkland and Harald Henrikssen are coming.
   Johan Meier isn't coming because he's too busy.
2 Speakers
   Jessica Langer is talking about Quality Management on Tuesday at 10.00.
   Thomas Salter is talking about Selling on Wednesday at 09.00.
   I don't have any confirmation from the other speakers.
3 Evening programme
   On Tuesday evening, we're going to the opera.
   On Wednesday evening, we're seeing a Shakespeare play at Stratford.

Please contact me if you have any more questions.
Best regards

Sounds good

Weak stress 2

1 Read the rubric and play track 25.3. Ask students for their opinions. Congratulate them if they can remember 'schwa' or at least the concept. Elicit or remind them of the way the schwa can make speech sound more rhythmic and natural and closer to a native speaker model. Then read the second rubric to confirm what you have just discussed.

Answer

Example 2 sounds more natural.

Track 25.3 tapescript ▶▶

1 When are you going to Romania?
2 When are you going to Romania?

2 Read the rubric and play track 25.4 for students to write down the questions. You may need to play it twice to give them time.
3 Play track 25.4 again and ask students to really focus on the rhythm of each question as they underline the schwas.

Answers and Track 25.4 tapescript ▶▶

A: What <u>are</u> you doing next week?
B: I'm going <u>to</u> Poland.
A: Pol<u>and</u>? What <u>are</u> you doing there?
B: I'm visiting <u>a</u> friend.
A: How long <u>are</u> you staying?
B: Just <u>for a</u> few days.
A: When <u>are</u> you coming back?
B: Next Friday.

A: <u>Are</u> you doing anything <u>at the</u> weekend?
B: Yes, I'm going camping.

4 Ask students to practise the dialogue in pairs and then change roles.

It's time to talk

The subject of this section is discussing future plans. Students have to consult the file cards at the back of the book in order to carry out the task. Notice (see Answer below) that there is in fact only one possible time when all the people in the situation are free to meet. Since the role-play involves a phone conversation, pairs may want to sit back-to-back.

Answer

The only time when three members of the management team can meet is on Wednesday morning.

What did we do today?

Check the Remember section quickly and remind students of the objectives of this lesson.

Follow up

Encourage students to:
1 consult their diaries to write sentences about their future plans using the present continuous with future reference
2 look for and note examples of this use of the present continuous in their professional or personal reading (for example, of graded readers).

26 Out of order

What did we do last time?

Do a review of the last type 2 lesson (Unit 23). Remind students of what they worked on (see Teacher's notes for that unit) and do some quick revision as follows.

Money and business finance vocabulary
Ask students to make sentences which show the meaning of verbs like *increase*, *decrease*, *pay*, *borrow* and *invest*. Ask them to define nouns like *turnover*, *profit*, *budget*, *margin* and *costs*.

Helping visitors
Ask students for some general phrases to use when helping visitors (like *Can I help?* and *Do you need any help?*). Then ask what they would say to a visitor who:
- needs a taxi
- wants help booking a theatre ticket
- wants to send an email
- has a flat mobile phone battery
- wants to buy a typical product from your region.

On the agenda: Why are we doing this?
Tell students the objectives of this lesson:
- to talk about **solving work problems**
- to learn useful **vocabulary for solving problems** (check their understanding of 'to solve a problem')
- to practise **solving problems by phone**.

Reinforce this by writing the key words on the board or OHP.

Warm up

First look at the two questions in the Student's Book and check understanding of *complain*. Get brief replies to these questions:
- When did it happen?
- Where did it happen?
- Why did it happen?
- Were you happy with the customer service you got after you complained?

Then look at the picture of Amy Harrison and read the caption. Ask students what an exhibition is – they can give examples of exhibitions (or 'trade fairs') they attend themselves – and what an exhibitions manager does. Explain that they are going to read about problems she had on a recent business trip to the USA.

Read on

Problems in Pennsylvania

1
- Read the rubric and the four questions. What do they think is the likely order before they read the paragraphs? (Difficult to say, this time!)
- When they have finished the skimming exercise, check their answers and ask them what key words or phrases helped them do the task (e.g. 'flight' in A, 'hotel' in B, '50% discount' in C, 'switched it on' in D).

> **Answers**
> 1 D 2 B 3 C 4 A

2 After checking the answers, ask students to summarise the four problems and responses in their own words. What should the hotel manager in paragraph B have done?

> **Answers**
> 1 She telephoned a travel agent friend.
> 2 It was overcooked and cold.
> 3 She forgot to switch it on.
> 4 A 25% discount

What do you think?

Do employees get training in customer care in the organisations where students work?
Do they have internal as well as external customers?
Can they give an example of how they handled a complaint?

The words you need ... to talk about work problems

1 You can write students' answers on the board as mindmaps with 'problem' in the middle and then invite them to develop it so that they build simple collocations like 'solve – a – difficult – problem', 'deal with – a – technical – problem', etc. Show them how collocational activities of this kind really help to build the bridge between individual words and sentences.

> **Answers**
> solve; tell (someone about); explain; deal with

2 Ask students to do the exercise and then check the answers. Ask them how many of these problems can be or have been problems for them as well. Can they suggest solutions to each problem?

> **Answers**
> 1 technical   2 time   3 time   4 technical   5 technical
> 6 time

3 You could also ask students to say what the problem could be (except number 4 where a problem is already given).

> **Answers**
> 1 You should / need to   2 You should / need to   3 Try
> 4 You need   5 Try   6 You need

It's time to talk

During feedback, invite each pair to tell the rest of the class what solutions they suggested for each problem. Write key phrases from them on the board and leave them – they may be helpful in the dialogue in the next section.

COMMUNICATING AT WORK

Telephoning 4: Solving problems by phone

1
> **Answers**
> 1 I'm having a problem
> 2 Could you get someone
> 3 I'll ask
> 4 Is that OK?
> 5 I didn't get
> 6 Could you send
> 7 I'll do
> 8 Call me back in 30 minutes if you still haven't got it.
> 9 I can't remember
> 10 Could you contact
> 11 I'll call
> 12 Do you want me to call back after I speak to him?

2

Track 26.1 tapescript ▶▶

Call 1

MARIA: Hi, Annie. It's Maria. I'm sorry but I'm having a problem with my computer.
ANNIE: What sort of problem?
MARIA: It keeps crashing for no reason. Could you get someone to check it?
ANNIE: Don't worry. I'll ask an engineer to check. Is that OK?
MARIA: Wonderful. Thank you. Bye.

Call 2

JULIE: Hello, Annie. It's Julie from Excom. I'm sorry but I didn't get the minutes from our last meeting.
ANNIE: Really? I sent them last week in an attachment.
JULIE: Well, I don't think they arrived. Could you send them again?
ANNIE: Sure. I'm really sorry about that. I'll do it now. Call me back in 30 minutes if you still haven't got it.
JULIE: That's great.

Call 3

PETER: Hi, Annie. It's Peter. I can't remember the time of our meeting next week.
ANNIE: Tuesday at 10 o'clock.
PETER: That's fine. Could you contact Jan? I forgot to tell him about it.
ANNIE: Of course. I'll call him straightaway. Do you want me to call back after I speak to him?
PETER: No, only call back if you don't reach him.

3 Remind students of possibly useful phrases on the board from the previous section. As you go round monitoring the activity, write up more phrases that you hear.

What did we do today?

Check the Remember section quickly and remind students of the objectives of this lesson.

Follow up

Encourage students to:
1. write down as many useful phrases for solving problems as possible that they can remember from this lesson
2. write a dialogue between a customer with a complaint and someone who is good at dealing with customers' problems.

27 Teaching T'ai Chi

What did we do last time?

Do a review of the last type 3 lesson (Unit 24). Remind students of what they worked on (see Teacher's notes for that unit) and do some quick revision as follows.

Talking about money

Ask students to make phrases including words like *lend*, *change* (as a verb and as a noun), *borrow*, *cash*, *cash point* and *commission*.

Money and shopping

Ask them to make sentences using verbs like *spend* (on), *save*, *invest* (in), *pay* (for), *buy* and *lend*. Insist on their using the right prepositions (as given in brackets).

On the agenda: Why are we doing this?

Tell students the objectives of this lesson:
- to practise useful phrases for **making invitations** (check that students understand this word)
- to learn and practise useful vocabulary for talking about **health and keeping fit**.

Reinforce this by writing the key words on the board or OHP.

Warm up

- Before you look at the Warm-up questions, explain that the unit title and the backdrop photo relate to the main subject of the unit and that you'll look at them in a little while.
- There is a potentially interesting intercultural dimension to these questions which you may be able to explore briefly. In some national and professional cultures, people socialise with colleagues outside work, in others not. In some, invitations are to someone's home; in others, they are to a restaurant. (But be careful not to seem to be too inquisitive about people's private lives.)

Inviting

Answers

| 1 e | 2 d | 3 b | 4 c | 5 j | 6 f | 7 g | 8 h | 9 a | 10 i |

Track 27.1 tapescript ▶▶

Inviting someone

SUE: Vasili, I'd like to invite you to lunch tomorrow after our meeting.
VASILI: Oh, thank you very much.
SUE: There's a Mexican restaurant nearby. Is that OK for you?
VASILI: That sounds good.
SUE: Good. I'll reserve a table.

Saying 'maybe' to an invitation

SUE: We're having a little party at the weekend. Can you and Jitka come?
BERNDT: That sounds nice. Thank you. But I'll have to check with Jitka.
SUE: Fine. Can you let me know before Friday?
BERNDT: I'll let you know before then.

Saying 'no' to an invitation

SUE: Michel, I want to try the new vegetarian café across the road. Are you free for lunch on Friday?
MICHEL: I'm afraid I can't. I have some visitors from the US. But thanks for the invitation.
SUE: That's OK. Another time.
MICHEL: Definitely.

Cancelling an invitation

VASILI: I'm really sorry Sue, but I have to cancel lunch tomorrow. Something's come up.
SUE: No problem.
VASILI: Can we fix another time?
SUE: Let's do something next week.
VASILI: Yes, sorry about that.

Have a go

Can students role-play other situations involving invitations – to a different kind of event, accepting or refusing?

Background briefing

T'ai Chi or T'ai Chi Ch'uan, to the casual observer, involves learning a sequence of physical movements which, when practised regularly, brings balance to the mind as well as to the body. T'ai Chi is not just a mild form of physical exercise, however. (Indeed, anyone who has tried it will testify that not only does it require huge concentration but is, for the uninitiated, extremely physically demanding.) The study of T'ai Chi Ch'uan in fact marks the historical meeting of many centuries of Taoist study known as Chi Kung ('Excellence of Energy'), which was primarily dedicated to physical health and spiritual growth, with the need of the time (approximately 1,000 AD) for Chinese monks to defend themselves against bandits and warlords. The result was, and is, a unique blend of healing, and of martial and meditative art.

T'ai Chi places great emphasis on mental and energy levels. The first quality to be developed in T'ai Chi is that of strengthening one's concentration, or what is referred to in the martial arts as being centred. The ability to centre the mind is really that of keeping the mind interested and involved in the experience of the present moment. This is understood to be the foundation of T'ai Chi because from this state of attention comes the possibility to change, correct, and heal. Unlike the prevailing Western view that one must work hard for the experience we call being healthy, in T'ai Chi health is understood to be natural (and therefore effortless) to that individual who has achieved balance and harmony between body and mind.

The essence of T'ai Chi practice is not to learn a set of movements, nor to become talented in a system of self-defence, although these abilities may occur during the course of practice. The intention of T'ai Chi is to allow one the opportunity to become more aware of the natural laws which govern change; not just change in the body as affects physical, structural movement, but rather principles of change and movement that govern every aspect of our lives and the world around us. The exercises of the practice simply provide us with an opportunity to explore that process of discovery.

With kind permission of Ron Perfetti: www.ronperfetti.com

Listen to this

T'ai Chi can improve your life

Look at the photo on the first page of the unit. Ask students to describe what they see and to say what they know about T'ai Chi: what is it? Why do people do it? Then look at the pictures of Mike Tabrett and read the caption.

Answers
1   1 T   2 F   3 T   4 F

2 After the exercise, discuss the questions with your students. Do they take two minutes to relax? What do they do to relax – if anything – in the middle of a busy day?

Answers
1 Meditation
2 You feel good / less stressed.
3 It makes you think about your health and your body.
4 Relax and breathe slowly.

Track 27.2 tapescript ▶▶

INTERVIEWER: Mike, what is T'ai Chi?
MIKE: T'ai Chi is not Kung Fu or anything like that. The idea of T'ai Chi is very different, it's internal. There are four main elements: firstly, working on the way we breathe; secondly, our body position; thirdly, learning soft movements to help energy and balance; and the final element is meditation, a quiet part, which many people like.
INTERVIEWER: And who comes to your classes?
MIKE: Anybody can come and do it. I have every type of person, from ten years old and I think my oldest student is about 90. All types, all physical types can benefit.
INTERVIEWER: So what are the benefits of T'ai Chi?
MIKE: Well, the main benefit is you just feel good, less stressed. T'ai Chi just helps you to be happier with your life.
INTERVIEWER: And is T'ai Chi better than other things you can do, like sport or being a vegetarian?
MIKE: I'm a vegetarian too but I think T'ai Chi is better than sport because it really makes you think more about your health, and you begin to know what is good and bad for the body. And so for many, T'ai Chi is a beginning and you go on and maybe run a marathon or do some other sporting activities. I think T'ai Chi makes you think – and that's good.
INTERVIEWER: Do you go to companies to do this kind of thing?
MIKE: A little, yes, at some business conferences. And I do stress management courses using T'ai Chi principles. And you can get good results. A simple thing I often say is that you should take two minutes, only two minutes, in the middle of a busy day, just to relax and breathe slowly. Breathing slowly can stop stress and so build energy again for the day.
INTERVIEWER: Can you say in one sentence why I should do T'ai Chi?
MIKE: Why should you do it? Well, it's easy. You should do T'ai Chi because I think it can improve your life!

The words you need ... to talk about health

1 You could ask students to describe the illustrations before doing the exercise.

Answers
1 e   2 c   3 a   4 b   5 f   6 d

2 After checking this and dealing with the questions, you can ask what advice they would give anyone with each of these six problems. For example:
• You could try . . .
• You could think about . . . -ing . . .
• Why don't you . . . ?

Answers
1 lose   2 stop   3 do   4 reduce   5 relax   6 go

Unit twenty-seven 71

It's time to talk

- Read the rubric and make sure students understand the task.
- Read through the Health action list to check understanding. The prices have been deliberately mismatched with the total figure available so that students have to find creative ways of rounding up or down the total which they arrive at.
- Ask them to work in pairs or groups of three and to choose one person to report back to the class with reasons for their decisions (what and why).

What did we do today?
Check the Remember section quickly and remind students of the objectives of this lesson.

Follow up
Encourage students to:
1 imagine they are writing healthy resolutions for the New Year. What three or four resolutions would they write?
2 write a short report from the organisation's health centre about ways in which employees can live healthier lives.

28 Perfect planning

What did we do last time?
Do a review of the last type 1 lesson (Unit 25). Remind students of what they worked on (see Teacher's notes for that unit) and do some quick revision as follows.

Future plans
Ask students questions like:
- What are you doing this evening?
- What are you doing at the weekend?
- What are you doing next week?

Ask them for the name of the tense they are using and about the uses they now know for it.

Weak stress
- Ask the students to repeat some of the questions you've just asked so that you can write them on the board. Did they use weak stress for *are* and *you*?
- Ask them to say them again while paying proper attention to weak stress and to tell you which syllables receive only weak stress.
- Ask them for other questions – not necessarily about future plans – beginning with words like *how much, how long, how far*, etc. Again, get them to focus on weak stress as they say them.

On the agenda: Why are we doing this?
Tell students the objectives of this lesson:
- to learn about the **present perfect tense**. Ask students if they recognise the name of this tense and if they know how it is formed. Write the form of a regular verb on the board, e.g. *I have learned, She has finished.*
- to talk about **organising things at work** and to practise **small talk**
- to work on **spelling and pronunciation**.

Reinforce this by writing the key words on the board or OHP.

Warm up
- The questions in the Student's Book can be approached either in terms of simple grammar drilling or in terms of a brief communicative activity, depending on how familiar your students already are with the present perfect and how they prefer to work. If they have met it before, they should be able to offer replies (e.g. to the first question) like: *Yes, I have, I've learned about our new . . .*
If not, you may initially need to provide model answers as follows:

Q: Have you learned something* today?
A: Yes I have. I've learned about . . .
Q: Have you enjoyed your work today?
A: Yes, I have. I've had an interesting meeting with . . .

*For the grammatically astute who may remember that 'any' is often used rather than 'some' in questions, you can tell them that the use of 'something' here simply suggests a question about one thing.

- Then look at the picture of Anne and read the caption. Explain that you're going to practise using the present perfect to talk about what has happened at work in the recent past and about our life experiences.

Listen to this

Have you organised everything?

> **Answers**
> **1** The taxi is for 10 am
> The Italia Sports meeting is on Thursday
> Dinner with Giulia is on Wednesday evening

2 You could also ask students to note down examples of the present perfect that they hear or to identify them from the tapescript. Can they say why the speakers are using the present perfect tense?

> **Answers**
> 1 T   2 F   3 T   4 F

Track 28.1 tapescript ▶▶

JANE: Hi, Anne. How are the plans for the exhibition going?
ANNE: I'm busy, but OK.
JANE: Good. Can I just check a few things? Have you booked the Hilton? I liked it there last time.
ANNE: Yes, I have, and I've asked for rooms with a sea view.
JANE: Great. What about getting to the airport? Have you booked the taxi?
ANNE: Yes, the taxi will pick us up from the office at ten.
JANE: Have you emailed Giulia to cancel the meeting yet?
ANNE: Oh, no. Sorry, not yet. But I've booked La Riviera for Wednesday evening to have dinner with her. I've read that the food is superb and they do fabulous risotto there.
JANE: Great. But could you email her today to confirm?
ANNE: OK, I'll do that immediately. And can I check something? I've organised your meeting with Italia Sports for Thursday. Is that OK?

JANE: Great. Now we can enjoy the trip. Have you ever been to Sicily?
ANNE: No, I haven't but I can't wait. I think it'll be great. Have you?
JANE: Yes, I've been to Sicily twice. The first time was quite romantic …

What do you think?

These questions could provoke lively debate. They involve other issues like:
- Do managers need secretaries? What for? (to deal with all their emails?)
- What's the difference between a secretary and a PA?

But don't let discussion go on for very long.

Check your grammar

The present perfect

Read the rubric and first give some of your own examples of what's happened (or what hasn't happened) at work. For example:
- I've taught three classes today.
- I've looked at my emails.
- I haven't called X about Y yet.

Ask students for, say, one sentence each about things they've done so far today.

Then give a couple of your own examples of experiences and what you've done in life. For example:
- I've visited China three times.
- I've never been in a car accident.

Ask students for one similar example each, then ask them to do the gap-fill exercise.

> **Answers**
> 1 booked 2 haven't 3 Has 4 been 5 have 6 hasn't

Do it yourself

- First do a quick check on irregular participles. As before, students who have encountered the present perfect before may well have rote-learned a number of irregular forms at some stage in the past and still be able to recall them, even if they are unsure about usage.
- Elicit or provide some basic irregular forms like *been*, *done*, *seen*, *had*, etc.
- Point out that *I've (never) been to China* = *I've (never) visited China*.
- Refer students to the list of irregular verbs in the Grammar reference section of the Student's Book. They may need to refer to it as they do these exercises.

> **Answers**
> 1 1 I've done it. / I did it last week.
>   2 She hasn't finished the report.
>   3 Have you (ever) been to Italy?
>   4 I haven't received any emails so far today.
>
> 2 2 has ordered   6 haven't told
>   3 has he ordered   7 have you spoken to
>   4 have also agreed   8 've never sold / have never sold
>   5 Have you told   9 has been

Track 28.2 tapescript ▸▸

ANNE: I've got some good news for you. We've received three big new orders. Bob Martin of TXL has ordered our Apollo sports shoe.
JANE: That's excellent. How many has he ordered?
ANNE: Three thousand! Great, isn't it! And ABC and Harcom Sports have also agreed to buy a thousand of our Eagle sports shirts.
JANE: Fantastic. Have you told Peter yet? He'll be delighted.
ANNE: No, I haven't told him yet. I'll phone him later this afternoon.
JANE: And have you spoken to any Japanese buyers?
ANNE: Yes, but no luck! In fact, we've never sold any of our products in Japan. But, despite that, I have to say that the exhibition has been a great success.
JANE: Thanks very much, Anne.

3 Monitor the open pairwork exercise at the end of this section, note model language and provide feedback to the whole class.

Sounds good

Spelling and pronunciation

1 Ask students not just to identify the correct pronunciations and to practise them, but also to say what it is which makes them problematic, i.e.
   - *comfortable* contains one less syllable than the spelling suggests
   - *receipt* contains a silent letter.

   Can they think of other examples of either phenomenon? For example, *vegetable* in the first case, and *biscuit*, *psychology*, etc. in the second.

2 - Ask students to decide on the correct pronunciations in pairs or small groups. Don't comment on the versions they come up with.
   - Play track 28.4 for them to check, then ask them to provide the correct pronunciations. Were they right about them all?

Tracks 28.3 and 28.4 tapescripts ▸▸

See Student's Book.

It's time to talk

Dinner talk

This can be organised along cocktail party lines with students changing partners when you signal for them to do so. Ask them to take notes and provide feedback on what they found out about each other at the end of the exercise. You can take notes on questions and answers you hear and write models on the board. Pay special attention to good questions coming up under the 'Other' category.

What did we do today?

Check the Remember section quickly and remind students of the objectives of this lesson.

Follow up

Encourage students to:
1 keep a diary for a week with daily entries about things they've done or haven't done today
2 write sentences about their own life experiences or those of someone they know

3 start a record of words they find difficult to pronounce.

Encourage students to buy the *Cambridge Learner's Dictionary* so they can check the pronunciation of any common words in English – both US and British English pronunciations from the CD.

29 A changing world

What did we do last time?
Do a review of the last type 2 lesson (Unit 26). Remind students of what they worked on (see Teacher's notes for that unit) and do some quick revision as follows.

Solving problems
What responses would students give to customers with these problems?
- a hotel guest with no hot water in the shower
- a visitor who can't find his way back to reception
- a supplier whose invoice has not been paid
- a customer who bought the wrong size shoes in a shoe shop.

Perhaps students can also think of situations and appropriate responses.

You can also ask students to think of verbs (and adjectives) which collocate with *problem*.

Problem solving by phone
Unit 26 identified two things that customers should do and two things that the people dealing with them should do (see the Remember section of Unit 26). Can students remember what they are?

Customers should:
- explain the problem clearly and
- ask for help politely.

The people dealing with them should:
- show understanding and
- offer help quickly and politely.

Can students suggest phrases for explaining and dealing with problems?

On the agenda: Why are we doing this?
Tell students the objectives of this lesson:
- to talk about **change**
- to learn vocabulary for **describing increases and decreases**
- to **practise arranging meetings by email**.

Reinforce this by writing the key words on the board or OHP.

Warm up
Look at the picture of Frank and read the caption. Ask the Warm-up question. What are sales people like? What is different about their job?

Read on

A year in Germany
Look at the picture at the bottom of the page and read the caption. Check understanding of *fertiliser*. Explain that this is what Frank sells in Germany, and you are going to talk about a country where there have been big changes over the last 15 or more years. Have there been big changes in the students' country or countries as well?

1 When they have finished the exercise, check their answers and ask them what key words or phrases helped them do the task (e.g. 'I work in . . . ' in A, 'Last year was' in B, 'the economy in Germany' in C, 'jobs . . . eastern Germany' in D).

Answers
1 D 2 C 3 A 4 B

2 After checking their answers, ask them to find all the words in the four paragraphs which indicate upward and downward trends. Are they verbs, nouns or adjectives?

Answers
1 Unemployment in eastern Germany increased.
2 The price of some of Frank's products decreased a little last year.
3 Bayer's market share increased a little.
4 Frank's work has increased a lot.

What do you think?
If students disagree with the statement, ask them to complete the sentence in a different way. You might offer: The most important thing in business is:
- to keep ahead of the competition
- to have happy workers
- to have a job you love
- to have satisfied customers
- to make a profit.

The words you need ... to talk about change

1 Can students say why some sentences are in the past simple and some are in the present perfect?

Answers
1 d 2 c 3 a 4 e 5 b

2 Remind students to consult the list of irregular verbs in the Grammar reference section, if necessary.

Answers
1 decreased   2 has risen   3 fell   4 have increased
5 went up

It's time to talk
Read the instructions. Ask each pair to ask and answer questions first on their organisations and then on their countries. Ask the class for feedback on both.

74 Teacher's notes: Units 1–30

COMMUNICATING AT WORK

Emails 3: Arranging meetings by email

Before looking at this section in the Student's Book, can students suggest phrases for emails to fix meetings? Write (correct) suggestions on the board.

1 After the exercise, ask them if the style of writing is formal or informal. Since they all tend towards the informal or at least neutral, can they suggest formulae for saying the same thing more formally, for example to someone they don't know very well or at all.

Answers

1 1 c   2 d   3 a   4 b
2 1 meet   2 by   3 forward   4 can't   5 make

3 Ask students to work in pairs while you go round helping and checking. Write up the best phrases on the board.

What did we do today?
Check the Remember section quickly and remind students of the objectives of this lesson.

Follow up
Encourage students to:
1 find an article or diagram from a professional document, newspaper or magazine which describes some kind of trend and write a summary of it
2 write more practice emails proposing, agreeing to, rearranging or proposing alternative dates for meetings.

30 Jets and pets

What did we do last time?
Do a review of the last type 3 lesson (Unit 27). Remind students of what they worked on (see Teacher's notes for that unit) and do some quick revision as follows.

Invitations
Ask students to make invitations beginning with phrases like:
- Can you . . . ?
- Would you like to . . . ?
- Are you free . . . ?

Then ask them what you can say to accept an invitation. For example:
- That would be very nice.
- I'd love to.

Then ask them what you can say to refuse an invitation (with an excuse). For example:
- That would be very nice but I'm afraid I . . .
- I'm sorry. I . . .

Health and fitness
What advice can students offer you to deal with these problems?
- I'm overweight.
- I feel tired all the time.
- I always feel stressed.
- I smoke 30 cigarettes a day.
- I don't get home from work until 9 in the evening.
- I only have time to eat a hotdog or a hamburger at lunchtime.

On the agenda: Why are we doing this?
Tell students the objectives of this lesson:
- to talk about **work and lifestyle**: you are going to talk about the different ways in which people with very different jobs lead their lives
- to learn **vocabulary about learning**
- to practise **saying goodbye** (as is appropriate for the last unit of the book). You can explain that, because of this, you will do the social English dialogues at the end of the lesson rather than at the beginning.

Reinforce this by writing the key words on the board or OHP.

Warm up
Ask students to:
- talk about each person's job and say which job each of them would prefer most and least
- describe something of the job of each person.

Listen to this

Working with animals

Ask students to describe the picture of Gayle Martz and read the caption.

Answers

1 1 T   2 T   3 F   4 T

2 1 She couldn't find a travelling bag for her dog, Sherpa.
   2 Four million dollars
   3 A good learner
   4 She does yoga.

Track 30.1 tapescript ▶▶

INTERVIEWER: So, Gayle, it's good to meet you. Can you tell me what you do?

GAYLE: Well, I have my own business, which is designing, making and selling products for travelling with a pet. OK, so what I do is pet travel.

INTERVIEWER: How did you get this idea?

GAYLE: Well, I changed my lifestyle totally. At the beginning, I was a flight attendant and I travelled all over the world. And then someone gave me a dog called Sherpa but I couldn't take her with me on airplanes. There just wasn't a bag anywhere in the world.

INTERVIEWER: OK, so, that's how you got the idea, and so then you went and started a business?

GAYLE: Well, what I did was some research and then I designed a bag and started to work with a company in Korea on the first, original Sherpa bag.

INTERVIEWER: Tell me a little about the business, how big you are, how many bags you sell, that kind of thing?
GAYLE: Well, I started in 1990 with one thousand bags and now I sell over one hundred thousand a year. And the Sherpa bag is now the standard for travel really in the world I think. So, it's gone from nothing to a four-million dollar company.
INTERVIEWER: That's fantastic. I guess you had to learn a lot in a short time!
GAYLE: It was difficult at first but, you know, we are learning things all through our life and I always try to be a good learner, and to learn interesting things.
INTERVIEWER: So, are you happy you have changed your lifestyle so much? You must be very busy.
GAYLE: Yes, it's very busy. But I'm really happy I've changed. Business is exciting! And if you do something you love, you will have success.
INTERVIEWER: So, with this busy lifestyle, can you still balance life and work?
GAYLE: Sure. You know, I was born and raised on the west coast, in California, and it's a very healthy lifestyle out there. I eat well, a lot of vegetarian food, that kind of thing. But what is really important to me now is yoga. Yoga helps you to relax, it gives you that balance; it is really a part of my life now. Everyone needs to have balance in their lives.

What do you think?

Point out the important phrase 'work–life balance' and ask these questions:
- If students would like to change, how would they like to change?
- We are all better at learning some things than others. What do students find it easy and difficult to learn about languages? Computer skills? Money management? Their feelings?

The techniques you need ... for learning vocabulary

Read the rubric and ask students:
- how many English words they think they know
- how many words they have learnt during the course
- what techniques they use for storing and memorising vocabulary. Tell them what techniques you use for the languages you have learnt or are learning.

Explain that they are going to look at three techniques for learning vocabulary.
Ask students to do exercises **1** to **3** and check the answers. Ask them to put the three techniques into order of preference for them personally.

Answers
1 Work: C   Internet: A   Health: B
2 1 a meeting   2 money   3 emails   4 a car
3 1 organised   2 organisation   3 organise

It's time to talk

Ask students to work in pairs. Can they add their own ideas to the list? You can add: Start *English365* Book 2 soon! Quite detailed reporting back will be useful here because students can broaden the range of their own learning strategies by learning about other people's. Try and convince students of the importance of studying little and often: even five minutes a day will bring them clear benefits over time. Can they make you – and themselves – a promise to keep to their action plan?

Saying goodbye

Answers
1 c   2 d   3 h   4 j   5 g   6 f   7 i   8 e   9 a   10 b

Track 30.2 tapescript ▶▶
Organising airport transport
A: Linda, when are you leaving?
B: I've ordered a taxi for 1 o'clock.
A: I'm leaving the office early. I can take you to the airport, if you want.
B: That's very kind but I can take a taxi. It's no problem.

Exchanging contact information
A: Here's my business card.
B: Oh, thanks, I'm afraid I don't have one with me.
A: Don't worry.
B: But this is my mobile number and email address.
A: Great. I'll contact you on Monday with the information you want.

Giving a present
A: Before you go, this is for you.
B: What's this?
A: It's a little present to say thank you.
B: It's beautiful. Thank you very much.
A: My pleasure. Thank you.

Saying goodbye
B: I have to go. The taxi's here.
A: Well, it was nice working with you.
B: Yes, the same for me. It was great.
A: Have a good trip back.
B: See you soon, I hope.
A: Take care. Bye.

Have a go

What did we do today?
Check the Remember section quickly and remind students of the objectives of this lesson.

Follow up
Encourage students to:
1 write down their action plan for learning English
2 review the organisation of their vocabulary learning book to see if there are other categories to add to it – for example, by theme, part of speech, collocation, etc.

Revision 2 Units 16–30

Answers

Grammar

1 1 What do you do?
   2 Where are you staying?
   3 What are you doing tonight?
   4 Have you been to Edinburgh before?
   5 When did you go? / When was that? / When were you last here?

2 1 have increased   2 has risen   3 fell   4 have stayed
   5 has gone up   6 went down

3 1 much   2 a few   3 many

4 1 should   2 have to / should   3 don't have to

General vocabulary

1 1 meat   2 a dessert   3 dish   4 wine list
   5 main course   6 bill

2 1 spend   2 save   3 borrow   4 lend   5 pay   6 get

Business communication

1 1 thanks   2 apologise   3 agenda   4 forward
   5 wishes

2 1 fix   2 discuss   3 convenient   4 what   5 confirm
   6 see

Pronunciation

1 1 45
   2 154
   3 338
   4 £4.99
   5 $99.50
   6 €565
   7 €30,000
   8 $65,500
   9 $250,000
   10 €1,500,000

Track R2.1 tapescript ⏭

   1 forty-five
   2 a hundred and fifty-four
   3 three hundred and thirty-eight
   4 four pounds ninety-nine
   5 ninety-nine dollars fifty
   6 five hundred and sixty-five euros
   7 thirty thousand euros
   8 sixty-five thousand five hundred dollars
   9 two hundred and fifty thousand dollars
   10 one million five hundred thousand euros

2 A: Are you staying for two or three days?
   B: I'm planning to stay for three days.
   A: Where are you staying?
   B: I'm staying at Vanna's house.
   A: Have you been to Italy before?
   B: I've been lots of times before!

Track R2.2 tapescript ⏭
See Student's Book.

Business vocabulary

1 turnover   2 costs   3 finance   4 budget   5 profit
6 margin

Social phrases

1 1 d   2 e   3 b   4 f   5 a   6 c

2
   2 B: Before you go, Annette. This is a little present just to say thank you.
   3 A: Oh, my favourite chocolates. Thank you very much.
   4 B: My pleasure.
   5 A: I shall eat these on the plane. OK, Ian, thank you again for everything.
   6 B: No problem. It was good to have you here.
   7 A: Take care. See you next month.
   8 B: Yes. Have a good trip. Bye.

4 Extra classroom activities

Teacher's notes

Introduction
There are 30 photocopiable activities designed to supplement each of the 30 units in the Student's Book in this section. Each activity is supported by some Teacher's notes. There are various possibilities as to when to do them:

- instead of the *It's time to talk* section of the unit
- in addition to and following *It's time to talk* – especially if your lessons are more than 90 minutes long
- as consolidation in the following lesson
- as consolidation later on in the course: you may want to use one if or when a natural break arises in a subsequent lesson.

However, do bear in mind that, unlike the Better learning activities, there is a direct link between the 30 Extra classroom activities and the 30 units in the Student's Book. Each Extra classroom activity should be used to reinforce and consolidate learning which has already been initiated and your lesson planning should take this into account.

Procedure
Most of the activities involve pair or groupwork of some kind, so before you do any of these activities, you should read, in particular, the notes on:
- pair and groupwork on page 16, and
- feedback and correction on page 17.

Timing
We have not indicated timings for individual activities because this will finally depend on you, your class and the time available. Do note, however, that:
- some of them are essentially supplementary exercises which will only take 10 to 15 minutes to do in normal circumstances; others are quite developed communicative activities which could take considerably longer
- you should assess how much time you think an activity will take, and how much you want it to take, at the planning stage. You may wish to spend as much if not more time on the feedback as on the activity itself.

What to do
See the Teacher's notes for each activity. Answers are also given in this section.

1 Who am I?
- You can ask students to do this activity as an extension of, or as a substitute for, *It's time to talk*. Or you can do it as consolidation of your Unit 1 work in a later lesson. It's intended as a quite light-hearted activity, like Charades, where the profile students build up doesn't necessarily hang together very well.
- Treat this as a serial pairwork activity (see page 16). Ask students to reverse roles, try the exercise without looking at the questions, adding questions and their own answers, etc.

2 Me and my organisation
- The photocopied page needs to be cut in half, one half for each Student A and the other half for each Student B.
- Introduce the activity, and suggest the usefulness of phrases like *I look after* . . . Students could imagine they are meeting each other at a cocktail party or a conference.
- Give students time to prepare questions. They are not new for them and are all very important, but some of them are difficult to formulate, so this is very useful consolidation work. Go round the class checking. You might like to put As and Bs together for this or work as a whole group. The questions that you hope the students will arrive at are:

  1. Who do you work for?
  2. What does your organisation do?
  3. Is it a big or a small organisation?
  4. Is it public or private?
  5. How many people work for your organisation?
  6. Where do you work?
  7. What do you do?
  8. What are your main responsibilities?
  9. What do you like about your job?
  10. What don't you like about your job?

- Good students will ask other questions to find things they have in common with each other so ask: *Did you ask any other questions*? during the feedback.
- After the activity, ask students to provide you with the information about their partners from their notes. For additional practice, they could then reverse the roles.

3 A perfect weekend
- Explain the situation and give time to each student to write down a list of weekend activities. Help with vocabulary as students work on their own. You could also give this to students to prepare for homework.
- Form pairs and encourage students to formulate questions in the present simple. In addition to the basic question: *What do you normally do on . . . ?*, encourage them to ask supplementary questions each time. This is an essential skill to develop in social communication, for example:
  A: What do you do on Saturday morning?
  B: I go swimming in my Olympic swimming pool.
  A: Do you like swimming? Where is your pool? Do you swim in the winter too? etc.
- Get feedback on the different weekends so that students can share their ideas with the rest of the class.

4 Daily routines

- Students can work in pairs to produce the most interesting new life for Brian. Do you need to remind them to use the third person *-s* when they report to the class?
- Pairs could read out alternate sentences about the new routine. Insist on grammatical and lexical accuracy and encourage others to spot any problems.

5 Alphabet soup

You can organise this as a competition. First allow pairs to work together to do the matching, decide on the meanings of each set of letters (BBC = British Broadcasting Corporation, etc.) and how to say the letters. Then as you check the answers with the whole class, give one point for each correct answer so that the maximum number of points scoreable is 3 x 15 = 45 points.

Answers

1	ABC	j) The alphabet: A – B – C
2	BBC	l) A British radio and TV company: the British Broadcasting Corporation
3	CNN	g) An American TV company: Cable News Network
4	DVD	n) Video on disk: digital video (or versatile) disk
5	EU	k) A group of countries with its headquarters in Brussels: The European Union
6	GB	h) An English-speaking country: Great Britain
7	H_2O	m) The chemical formula for water: hydrogen dioxide
8	Jan	b) The first month of the year: January
9	km	f) A measure of distance: kilometre
10	LA	c) A city on the west coast of the USA: Los Angeles
11	mph	o) The speed that British people drive at: miles per hour
12	R & D	e) A company needs this to develop new products: Research and Development
13	TV	d) People watch it: television
14	UK	h) The same English-speaking country: the United Kingdom (which includes Northern Ireland)
15	WWW	a) The start of a website address: World Wide Web

6 The place where I live

This could be managed as a pyramid exercise with a large class, i.e. first ask pairs to agree on an order of priority, then (without forewarning them) ask two pairs to agree together; then get two groups of four to agree together until they have a list to present to you which has been agreed by the whole class (more or less!). Otherwise ask each pair to present their list – they could write them on the board – and to give reasons for their choices.

7 My workplace

- This can be handled as a classic pairwork activity. Students can use their imaginations to describe the place where they would really like to work.
- Check understanding of the question *What is near the office?* This is intended to establish where students like to be near – green space or in the city centre with plenty of shops, restaurants, etc.

8 My ideal manager

- This activity extends the *It's time to talk* activity in Unit 8 in the Student's Book so can be done as an extension or as an alternative to this. All of the words in the input section are from the unit in the Student's Book although you should check understanding of *ideal*.
- There are more than the usual number of tasks (see *What to do*), so go through these with the students and make sure they understand them all.

Answers

The opposites are:
organised – disorganised
patient – impatient
hard-working – lazy
popular – unpopular
positive – negative
relaxed – stressed

9 London and New York

- Cut the photocopiable page in half and give one to each student in the pair.
- Encourage students to make sentences like:
  New York/London is: exciting/boring noisy/quiet
  crowded/empty clean/dirty dangerous/safe
  cheap/expensive too big/too small hot/cold fast/slow
  beautiful/ugly because . . . !
- The true value of this activity is perhaps in the transfer because you can ask them to repeat the activity but this time presenting their own cities or cities they know particularly well, to each other.

10 Big or small?

Encourage students to make sentences like:
- You are freer in a small organisation than in a big organisation.
- You can have more responsibility in a big organisation than in a small organisation.
- No, I don't agree! etc.

After the activity, you can do a class survey of how many students prefer big to small and vice versa, and why.

11 Job satisfaction

This activity need not go on for very long and three or four jobs per student should be enough. Encourage students to include at least one choice of their own. You can manage the reporting back stage by asking for feedback on each job in turn.

12 Sports quiz

- Check that there are not too many seriously anti-sport students in the class!
- Explain to students that the quotations are typical references to each sport, not quotations by or about the stars.
- If students work in pairs, you can give them marks for each correctly placed star and quotation and award additional marks for giving information about the stars or providing extra vocabulary for any of the sports. They can use the extra space in the table to do this.
- When you check the answers, ask students to mime the actions for football, golf, swimming (all four strokes), and boxing.
- Finally, do a survey to find out which of these sports is the most popular and which is the least popular in the class.

Answers

Sport	Star		From the TV commentary
Football	10 Ronaldo	e	He headed a great goal from the corner kick.
Golf	6 Tiger Woods	g	It was a beautiful putt – three under par!
Athletics	8 Marion Jones	f	She should go under eleven seconds if she runs like that again on the big day.
Swimming	9 Ian Thorpe	h	His favourite event is the individual medley – backstroke, butterfly, breaststroke and freestyle.
Skiing	4 Jean-Claude Killy	c	He's very strong in the alpine events – Downhill, Slalom and Giant Slalom.
Cycling	1 Lance Armstrong	a	He won the last three stages of the Tour and is now wearing the yellow jersey.
Boxing	5 Lennox Lewis	d	He knocked him out in the third round with an uppercut to the jaw.
Basketball	2 Michael Jordan	i	He was penalised for travelling with the ball and so they won the game by one point.
Sailing	7 Ellen MacArthur	j	She is the favourite to win this year's solo round-the-world yacht race.
Tennis	3 Serena Williams	b	She won the set on a tie break after being 15–40 down in the last game.

13 Life stories

- Photocopy the page and give several copies to each student. Alternatively, just draw the table on the board and tell them to copy it for each new round of the game.
- Explain that the game has several rounds. Each round deals with a different famous person.
- Read out the first of the facts. If a student thinks he/she knows who the mystery person is, he/she whispers the answer to you and scores five points. If another student gets the answer right after the second question, he/she scores four points, etc. If a student guesses wrongly, he/she forfeits the points for the identity of the person for that round.
- Students get extra points for identifying the verb each time and correctly writing down whether it is regular or irregular.
- Material for six rounds is provided below. You can add your own and also invite students to provide material as well and to lead the class.
- Biographies you can use are:

Margaret Thatcher
1 She was born in 1925.
2 She studied chemistry and law at university.
3 She married a British company director.
4 She lost her job in 1990.
5 She was British Prime Minister from 1979 to 1990.

Pablo Picasso
1 He was born in Malaga in Spain.
2 He died in Mougins in the south of France at the age of 91.
3 He spent the Second World War in Paris.
4 He died in 1973.
5 He painted a famous anti-war picture called *Guernica*.

Nelson Mandela
1 He was born in Transkei in 1918.
2 He married Winnie Mdikizela in 1961.
3 He went to prison in 1964.
4 He joined the ANC in 1944.
5 He became President of South Africa in 1994.

William Shakespeare
1 He was born in 1564.
2 He died in 1616.
3 He was an actor and writer in London.
4 He married a woman called Anne Hathaway.
5 He spent the last years of his life in Stratford.

Charles Darwin
1 He was born in Shrewsbury, England in 1809.
2 He died in 1882.
3 He went on an expedition in 'The Beagle' from 1831 to 1836.
4 During the expedition, he visited the Galapagos Islands.
5 He wrote a book called *The Origin of Species*.

Julius Caesar
1 He was born in about 100 BC.
2 He did his first military service in Turkey in about 80 BC.
3 He started a war against Pompey in 49 BC.
4 He became a dictator in 44 BC.
5 He was killed in Rome in 44 BC.

14 The merger
- There is obviously no one right answer to this problem so students should be interested to see the different proposals during the reporting back stage.
- Check understanding of *merger*: when two organisations (for example, two companies) join together to make one bigger organisation, they *merge* (verb). This is a *merger* (noun).
- It could be helpful to have pairs draw their new organisation charts on an overhead transparency so they can present them straightaway to the rest of the group.
- Encourage students to use language such as:
  There are ... divisions.
  There are ... departments.
  The ... manager looks after ...
  The ... manager is responsible for ...
  There are ... people on the management committee.
  The ... is under the ...
  The ... answers to / reports to the ...

15 Holiday home
- Students have the opportunity to exercise their imagination in this activity or perhaps to base their ads on real locations. In any case, you might finish with a group verdict on the place where most people would like to spend a holiday.
- When students ask each other about their various homes, encourage them to use language such as:
  Does it have a ...?
  How far is it from ...?

16 What are they doing?
- This can be quite light-hearted and the enjoyment should come as much during the feedback session as during the pairwork activity.
- Write *What is happening?* and/or *What are they doing?* in big letters on the board and encourage students as far as possible to write the captions in the present continuous.

17 Workplace communication
- Check that students understand CEO (Chief Executive Officer).
- This activity is fairly transparent. If the class is not too big, you could ask students to agree on a common policy to present to the senior management.

18 National dishes
- Check understanding of *ingredient* before students begin.
- Listen in to pairwork and progressively build up a wordlist on the board. Keep the focus on ingredients rather than how to cook the dishes.
- Encourage students to suggest other national dishes, especially from their own country.
- This is also a good opportunity to practise names of countries and related adjectives, for example: *Goulash is from Hungary. It's a Hungarian dish.*

Answers

Caviar	Russsia and Iran
Curry	India and Pakistan
Goulash	Hungary
Hamburger	USA
Moussaka	Greece
Paella	Spain
Pasta	Italy
Profiteroles	France
Roast beef and Yorkshire pudding	England
Sushi	Japan
Sweet and sour pork	China

19 Cultural rules and recommendations
- Check that students understand *rules* and *recommendations*.
- Encourage them to write just one or two simple sentences for each heading in the information booklet. Feedback will be helped if they can write the sentences on a transparency or on a PC to project them on a computer screen.
- If students are all from the same country, compare ideas for each heading and decide for each heading which are the most important pieces of advice.

20 Computers in your life
- First give students time to read the questions and write down their own answers. Or set this as a homework task at the end of the previous lesson.
- Ask the students to interview two other people in the class. Keep a note of the time so they know when to reverse roles and when to change over.
- Then carry out a survey of the class's use of computers by asking for answers to each question in turn: note down the main ideas on the board, and ask individual students to summarise the answers for the class as a whole.

21 Dream hotel
- You could ask students to read the report for homework following the previous lesson though this is not essential. They should plan their questions for their partner.
- The report is in note form but encourage students to communicate with each other and to report back to the class using complete sentences.

22 Number work
- If possible, you should make two copies of the table for each student: one for the scrambled exercise on the page, and one for the pairwork exercise in which students invent their own numbers.
- Point out or elicit the alternative way of saying the time in this activity – *seven twenty-five*.

Answers

What it is	How you write it	How you say it
A figure	123,456	one hundred and twenty-three thousand, four hundred and fifty-six

A date	30.10.03	the thirtieth of October, two thousand and three
A phone number	00 44 1904 661683	double oh, double four, one nine oh four, double six, one six, eight three
A year	1789	seventeen eighty-nine
A price	€45.70	forty-five euros, seventy cents
An exchange rate	$1 = €1.05	one point oh five euros to the dollar
A percentage	99%	ninety-nine per cent
A time (twelve-hour clock)	7.25	twenty-five past seven
A time (twenty-four hour clock)	13.55	thirteen fifty-five (five to two)

23 It's my business

- Explain that the students should use their own names in the interview but that other information needs to be invented by Student B, so give the Bs a little time to go through the text and decide on a company name, activity, start-up date, turnover, size of start-up loan, profit, costs and future investment. Student As can do the same for when students reverse roles.
- You can also explain the double meaning in the activity title and present the phrase *It's none of your business.*

24 Shopping lists

You could also ask students if they can invent sentences from customers in other locations – a bank, a garage, a hairdresser, etc. – to test their colleagues. Or suggest places like these to them and ask them what customers might typically say in each.

Answers

1	Record store	h) Do you have the Bach Double Violin Concerto?
2	Baker	f) A large white and four small cakes, please.
3	Butcher	g) Four steaks and half a kilo of sausages, please.
4	Post office	b) How much is a letter to Martinique?
5	Jeweller	a) Do you have a smaller one? This one's too big for my finger.
6	Sports shop	i) I'd like some new shorts and a pair of size 41 boots.
7	Pharmacy	j) What can you give me for a headache and a bad cold?
8	Clothes shop	k) Can I try another one on? This one's too small.
9	Bookshop	e) Do you have the fifth *Harry Potter*?
10	Travel agency	d) I'd like five nights on the Costa del Sol for two in February.
11	Newsagent	c) The *FT*, *The Economist* and *Vogue*, please.

25 A busy schedule

- Divide the class into As and Bs. Both can draw up a schedule for the start because both will eventually play the role of the PA.
- Check understanding of *schedule* (which means approximately the same as 'timetable' or 'programme').
- Remind the executives (Bs) that they have to score the As on the number of times they use the present continuous.
- Bs have to listen out for a credible schedule over the three days. They should ask questions if they don't find the programme plausible.

26 Problems at work

- Students can do the quiz on their own first or can work with a partner.
- For some situations there is one choice which is obviously wrong, but there may be disagreement about which is best. Teachers may also disagree – Americans and British native speakers, for example, may have different stylistic preferences, while some teachers and students may argue that a fairly direct style is typical of and acceptable for international communication in English.

27 New Year resolutions

You could ask students during the feedback if they have any other suggestions for Jamie.

28 Executive star

Point out to students that, although not every question needs to be in the present perfect, many of the questions can be formed using this tense. Check that students are planning to do so at the preparation stage.

29 Forecasting the future

There will probably be general agreement on most of the trends, so look out for any contrary opinions during the feedback.

Answers

1 d 2 f 3 h 4 c 5 a 6 g 7 b 8 e

30 Lifestyles

Encourage students to report their answers along the following lines:
- Jeanette thinks living in a big city is best. (1)
- Her family is the most important thing in her life. (2)
- Her personal appearance is important to her. (3)
  etc.

1 Who am I?

Objective
To practise meeting people and talking about yourself.

Introduction
In this activity, you can be another person. In fact, you can be a number of different people. Just choose from the different answers to create a new you.

What to do
You are at a cocktail party. You meet several people (people in your class) who you don't know. Ask them these questions.

1 Hello. My name's .... What's your name?
2 Where do you come from?
3 Where do you live?
4 Where do you work?
5 Who do you work for?
6 What do you do?
7 Are you married?
8 Do you have children?
9 How much money do you earn?
10 What car do you drive?

Input

Name
Use your own name or one of these:
John Smith	Maria Santiago
Helmut Schmidt	Paula Baggio
Pierre Durand	Eva Svensson

Come from
Bermuda	Georgia
Iceland	Paraguay
Madagascar	Mongolia

Live in
Kathmandu	Addis Ababa
Medellin	Bangalore
Alexandria	Birmingham

Work in
London	Madrid
Paris	Rome
Berlin	Brussels

Work for
The government	Air France
The UN	Myself
The BBC	A big hotel group

Job
Secretary	Singer
Manager	Banker
Cook	Writer

Marital status
Married	Widowed
Single	Have a partner
Divorced	Engaged

Children
0	3
1	4
2	5

Money
A lot	A good salary
Too much	A poor salary
Not much	Next question, please.

Car
Mini	Renault
Rolls Royce	BMW
Chevrolet	Trabant

2 Me and my organisation

Objective
To use language for asking and answering questions about companies and organisations.

Introduction
In this activity, you will talk about jobs and organisations.

What to do (Student A)
You work for Perfect Parties. You are going to meet someone (your partner) who does a different job.
1 Write questions to get information about your partner's organisation, activity, etc.
2 Ask and answer each other questions and note your partner's answers.

Input

Name of organisation	Perfect Parties
Activity	Organises big parties for birthdays, etc.
Big/small	Small
Public/private	Private
Number of employees	4
Place	New York
Job	Party organiser
Responsibilities	Children's parties
Good things	Seeing people having fun
Bad things	Working every weekend – a lot of people have parties at the weekend!

✂ --

2 Me and my organisation

Objective
To use language for asking and answering questions about companies and organisations.

Introduction
In this activity, you will talk about jobs and organisations.

What to do (Student B)
You work for York District Hospital. You are going to meet someone (your partner) who does a different job.
1 Write questions to get information about your partner's organisation, activity, etc.
2 Ask and answer each other questions and note your partner's answers.

Input

Name of organisation	York District Hospital
Activity	Looks after people who are ill
Big/small	Quite big
Public/private	Public
Number of employees	About 1,000
Place	York
Job	Nurse
Responsibilities	Cardiovascular patients
Good things	Helping sick people to feel better
Bad things	Long hours; Sometimes working at night

3 A perfect weekend

Objective
To practise talking about free-time activities.

Introduction
In this activity, you will tell your partner about a perfect weekend.

What to do
You are a millionaire and so is your partner. You like your free time and you never work at weekends.
1 Write down what you do at weekends.
2 Ask your partner what he/she does. Write notes in the table.
3 Tell your partner what you do.

Input

	You	Your partner
Friday evening		
Saturday morning		
Saturday afternoon		
Saturday evening		
Sunday morning		
Sunday afternoon		
Sunday evening		
Monday morning		

4 Daily routines

Objective
To practise using time adverbs: *always*, *often*, *usually*, *sometimes*, *occasionally*, *rarely* and *never*.

Introduction
In this activity, you are going to talk about daily routines.

What to do
Brian has a very boring lifestyle. Read his diary. He does the same things every day. With a partner, change each sentence to make his day more exciting. For example:
- He never gets up before 11 o'clock.
- He always has lunch in an expensive restaurant.

Present Brian's new life to the rest of the class. Who can give him the best day?

Input

Brian's diary

Dear diary,
Here is my typical day. It's the same every day. What can I do to change?
I always get up at 7 o'clock.
I usually have cornflakes for breakfast.
I always go to work by bus.
I always get to work at 8.45.
I often have a cup of coffee when I get to work.
I usually check my emails three times a day.
I often have a meeting in the morning.
I rarely make more than three phone calls a day.
I never receive more than three phone calls a day.
I usually have lunch in the company restaurant.
I usually have a sandwich.
I never have a sleep after lunch.
I sometimes have a meeting with my boss in the afternoon.
I never spend the day outside the office.
I always leave work at 5 o'clock.
I always get home at 6 o'clock.
I always watch TV in the evening.

5 Alphabet soup

Objective
To practise your spelling in English.

Introduction
In this activity, you are going to:
- practise saying letters of the alphabet in English
- test your general knowledge – also in English!

What to do
Work with a partner.
1 Match the definitions (a–o) with the letters (1–15).
2 What do they stand for?
3 Can you say them?
When you finish, see if you have more correct answers than the other pairs.

Input

1	ABC	a) The start of a website address
2	BBC	b) The first month of the year
3	CNN	c) A city on the west coast of the USA
4	DVD	d) People watch it
5	EU	e) A company needs this to develop new products
6	GB	f) A measure of distance
7	H_2O	g) An American TV company
8	Jan	h) An English-speaking country
9	km	i) The same English-speaking country
10	LA	j) The alphabet
11	mph	k) A group of countries with headquarters in Brussels
12	R & D	l) A British radio and TV company
13	TV	m) The chemical formula for water
14	UK	n) Video on disk
15	WWW	o) The speed that British people drive at

6 The place where I live

Objective
To practise talking about the place where you live.

Introduction
In this activity, you are going to discuss with your partner what makes a town or city a good place to live in.

What to do
Work with a partner. Your job is to make a plan. You have a budget of €250m. Decide how you want to spend the money and decide the order of importance of the services you want. Then tell the rest of the class about your plan.

Input

You work in the planning department for your town, which has about 80,000 people. Your town is 50 kilometres from a big city with good services. Your town has offices and factories, a big shopping centre with cinemas, clubs and discotheques and a good road to the nearest city. But public services are not very good. The city does not have:

A sports centre (cost: €50m)

A big park (cost: €20m)

A theatre and a concert hall (cost: €80m)

A library (cost: €30m)

A museum (cost: €40m)

A hospital (cost: €200m)

Cycle ways (cost: €1m)

Good bus services (cost: €10m)

A recycling centre (cost: €10m)

Cheap flats and houses for families, old people and young people (cost: €70m)

Your ideas?

7 My workplace

Objective
To practise talking about the place where you work.

Introduction
In this activity, you are going to think about your perfect office and ask and answer questions about it.

What to do
You work in a perfect office.
- Think about your answers to the questions.
- Then answer your partner's questions about it and ask him/her about his/her perfect office.

Input

Office questionnaire

1 The office block

Where is the office?

Is it new or old?

How many floors are there?

What is near the office?

2 Your office

How big is your office? (in square metres)

What do you have in your office?

What can you see from your window?

3 Other facilities

Is the office equipment (computers, photocopiers, etc.) good? (give details)

Is there a restaurant? (give details)

Are there sports facilities? (give details)

Is there a car park for employees?

Is there a place for people to meet and talk?

Are tea and coffee free?

Is there a place for smokers?

What are the other good things about this workplace?

8 My ideal manager

Objective
To practise talking about people.

Introduction
In this activity, you are going to describe different kinds of people doing different kinds of job.

What to do
1. Which of the words below would you use to describe:
   - the ideal manager
   - the ideal secretary
   - the ideal teacher
   - the ideal student.

   Choose four or five words for each. Add your own words if you can. Tell your partner.
2. How many pairs of opposites can you find? How many other opposites do you know? Tell your partner.
3. Describe your ideal manager to your partner. Give all these details:
   Age
   Gender (male/female)
   Job
   Free-time interests
   Positive qualities (use words from the Input section)
   Good/excellent at . . .

Input

Look at words we use to describe people. Do you understand them all?

ambitious	hard-working	organised
competitive	impatient	patient
disorganised	late	popular
efficient	lazy	positive
energetic	negative	relaxed
enthusiastic	nice	stressed
friendly	on time	unpopular

9 London and New York

Objective
To practise talking about city life.

Introduction
In this activity you are going to talk about a major world city.

What to do (Student A)
1 Imagine you live in New York. Read the information and prepare to tell your partner about:
   • what you can see and do in your city
   • what is good about your city.
2 Ask your partner about his/her city.

Input

Places to see and things to do in New York

St Patrick's Day Parade	An Irish carnival on Fifth Avenue
The US Open	A tennis championship at Flushing Meadow
Madison Square Garden	Rock concerts
Macy's	A big store on Fifth Avenue
Chinatown	Restaurants
Broadway	Theatre
Central Park	Green space in the centre of the city
Museum of Modern Art (MOMA)	Modern art
The Empire State Building	For fantastic views of New York

✂--

9 London and New York

Objective
To practise talking about city life.

Introduction
In this activity you are going to talk about a major world city.

What to do (Student B)
1 Imagine you live in London. Read the information and prepare to tell your partner about:
   • what you can see and do in your city
   • what is good about your city.
2 Ask your partner about his/her city.

Input

Places to see and things to do in London

The Notting Hill Carnival	A big multicultural carnival
Highbury	Home of Arsenal Football Club
The Royal Festival Hall	Concerts of classical music
Harrods	A big store in Knightsbridge
Soho	Pubs, clubs and restaurants
The West End	Theatre
Hyde Park and Regent's Park	Green spaces in the centre of the city
Tate Modern	Modern art
Buckingham Palace	The Queen's home in London

10 Big or small?

Objective
To practise comparing.

Introduction
In this activity, you are going to talk about big and small organisations.

What to do
1 With your partner, put the reasons for working in a big or small organisation into the table.
2 Do you work for a big or a small organisation? Tell your partner why. Use the comparatives of the adjectives to help you.

Can you add words to the lists of adjectives and nouns?

Adjectives
free
friendly
good
flexible
interesting
boring
stressful

Nouns
pay
facilities
responsibility

Input

Reasons for working in big/small organisations
You can:
- know everyone in the organisation
- meet lots of different people in the organisation
- deal with problems face-to-face
- have rules for dealing with problems
- do lots of different jobs at the same time
- specialise
- feel that your work helps the organisation
- know that everyone knows your organisation.

Big organisations	Small organisations
Add your ideas here:	Add your ideas here:

English365 Book 1 © Cambridge University Press 2004

11 Job satisfaction

Objective
To practise talking about different jobs.

Introduction
In this activity, you are going to talk about the good and bad things about different jobs.

What to do
1 Choose one of the jobs. Tell your partner what the good things and the bad things are about this job.
2 Change roles.
3 Repeat the activity for other jobs.

Input

JOBS
Pilot
Writer
Doctor
Film actor
Secretary
Call centre employee
Train driver
Travel agent
Restaurant waiter/waitress
University teacher
Language trainer
Your own choice

Good and bad things about the job
Money
Hours (short/long)
Freedom
Workspace (home/office)
Colleagues
Personal and professional development
Meeting people
Interest
Stress
Travel

12 Sports quiz

Objective
To learn more vocabulary for sports and physical activities; to practise the language of sport.

Introduction
In this activity, you are going to test your knowledge of sport.

What to do
With a partner:
1 Match the sports, the stars (1–10), and the quotations from typical TV or radio commentaries (a–j) for these sports.
2 Most of the stars are men. Can you name other female stars for these or other sports?
3 Discuss which of these sports is the most popular and which is the least popular in your country.

Input

Sport	Star	From the TV commentary
Football		
Golf		
Athletics		
Swimming		
Skiing		
Cycling		
Boxing		
Basketball		
Sailing		
Tennis		

1 Lance Armstrong
2 Michael Jordan
3 Serena Williams
4 Jean-Claude Killy
5 Lennox Lewis
6 Tiger Woods
7 Ellen MacArthur
8 Marion Jones
9 Ian Thorpe
10 Ronaldo

a He won the last three stages of the Tour and is now wearing the yellow jersey.
b She won the set on a tie break after being 15–40 down in the last game.
c He's very strong in the alpine events – Downhill, Slalom and Giant Slalom.
d He knocked him out in the third round with an uppercut to the jaw.
e He headed a great goal from the corner kick.
f She should go under eleven seconds if she runs like that again on the big day.
g It was a beautiful putt – three under par!
h His favourite event is the individual medley – backstroke, butterfly, breaststroke and freestyle.
i He was penalised for travelling with the ball and so they won the game by one point.
j She is the favourite to win this year's solo round-the-world yacht race.

13 Life stories

Extra classroom activities

Objective
To practise listening to and using the past simple tense.

Introduction
In this activity, you are going to play a game based on the life stories of famous people.

What to do
1. Your teacher will give you a number of answer sheets.
2. He/she will then tell you five facts – one at a time – about a famous person, past and present. Use your answer sheet to make notes.
3. If you know who the person is after the first fact, signal to the teacher but don't say the answer. Your teacher will check your answer with you.
4. If you get the answer right after one fact, you score five points; after two, you score four points, etc.
5. You get an extra point if you write down the verb used for each fact and can say if it's regular or irregular. The winner is the student with the most points at the end of the game.

Input

	Your notes	The verb you hear	Regular or irregular?
1			
2			
3			
4			
5			
Total score:			

English365 Book 1 © Cambridge University Press 2004

14 The merger

Objective
To practise talking about organisations.

Introduction
In this activity, you are going to discuss how to merge two organisations into one.

What to do
You and your partner are business consultants. Your job is to help two organisations to become one. Both companies are in the same area of business. The new company should not have more than 90 people.
1 Decide on the new organisation with your partner. Make it as simple as possible. Have as few departments as possible.
2 Present the new organisation to the class.

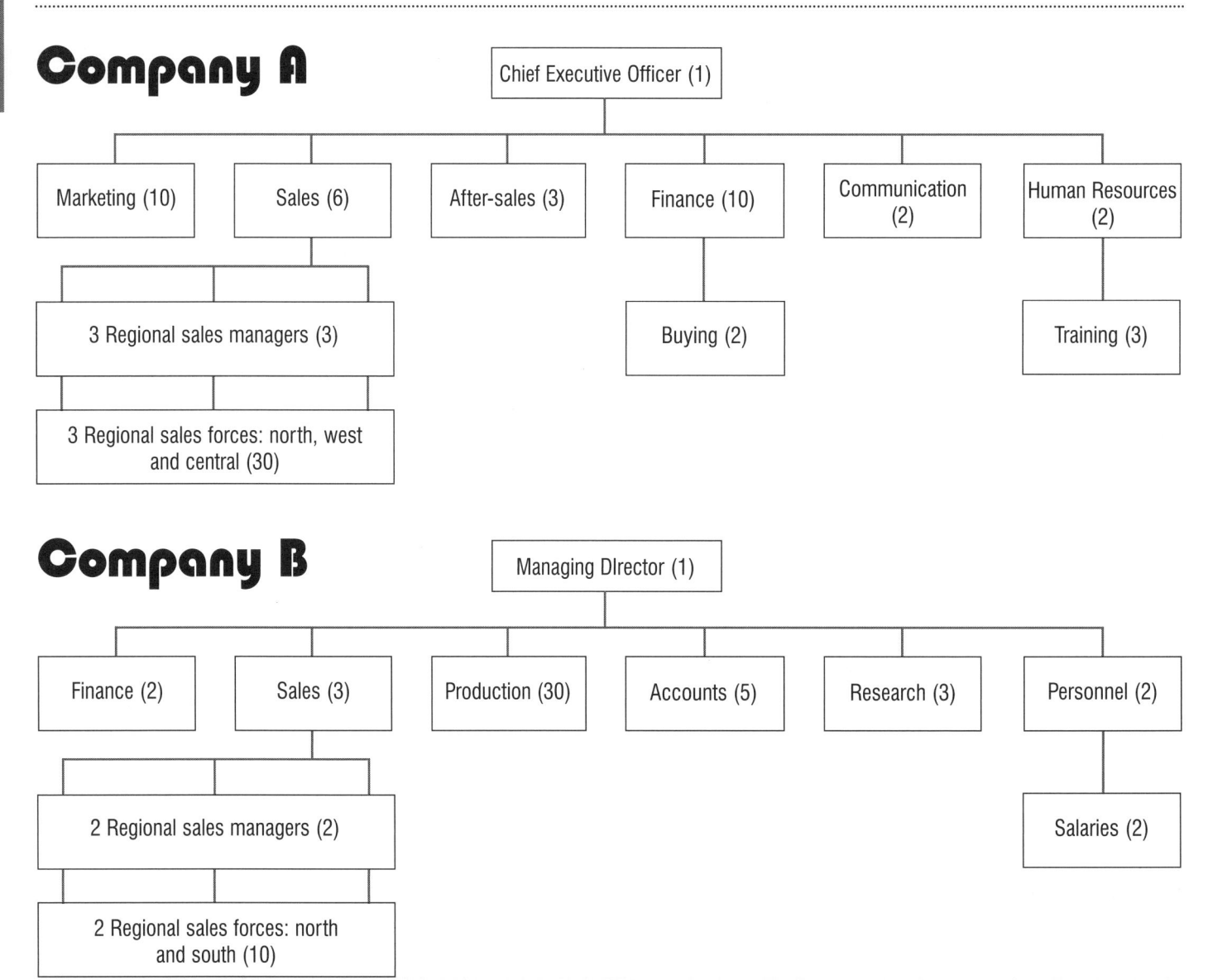

Input

Company A

- Chief Executive Officer (1)
  - Marketing (10)
  - Sales (6)
    - 3 Regional sales managers (3)
      - 3 Regional sales forces: north, west and central (30)
  - After-sales (3)
  - Finance (10)
    - Buying (2)
  - Communication (2)
  - Human Resources (2)
    - Training (3)

Company B

- Managing Director (1)
  - Finance (2)
  - Sales (3)
    - 2 Regional sales managers (2)
      - 2 Regional sales forces: north and south (10)
  - Production (30)
  - Accounts (5)
  - Research (3)
  - Personnel (2)
    - Salaries (2)

15 Holiday home

Objective
To practise talking about holiday homes and activities.

Introduction
In this activity, you are going to advertise a holiday home.

What to do
You and your partner are in the holiday business. You have a holiday home which you let to holidaymakers.
1. With your partner, write information about your home in the advertisement below. Use the advertisment on the right to give you ideas.
2. Present your holiday home to the class and answer their questions about it.

> Holiday cottage to let in the English Lake District. Easy to reach from Manchester Airport and by car (M6). Sleeps 6. Parking behind the house. Two floors. Ground floor: kitchen, dining/living room, single bedroom. First floor: two double bedrooms + single, bathroom. Wonderful views of the hills. Facilities: colour TV, dishwasher, washing machine, microwave, fridge. Large garden with children's play area. Great location for hill walking, riding, fishing and golf.
> Price (Oct–Mar): £450 p.w.
> (Apr–Sept): £650 p.w.

Input

- chalet / villa / cottage / flat
- by car / by train / by plane
- bedroom / bathroom / dining room / kitchen
- TV / heating / dishwasher / washing machine
- garden / swimming pool / play area / water sports
- hills / beaches / countryside
- golf / fishing / walking / swimming / sightseeing tours
- nearest village / town / city
- shops / museums / castles / country houses

Can you add to the list?

HOLIDAY HOME TO LET

Country:

Region:

How to get there:

Sleeps (number):

Parking:

Description of the house:

Description of the area:

Local attractions:

Price (low season):

Price (high season):

16 What are they doing?

Objective
To practise using the present continuous tense.

Introduction
In this activity, you are going to write captions for a series of pictures.

What to do
1 With your partner, write down your captions to the ten pictures.
2 Compare your captions with the others in the class.

Input

WHAT ARE THEY DOING?

1 What? Why?
She's buying an umbrella because the weather is terrible.

2 Who to? What about?

3 Where? What?

4 Where to? Why?

5 Who? Where?

6 What? Why?

7 Why?

8 Who? Where?

9 What? What about?

10 What kind? Where?

98 English365 Book 1 © Cambridge University Press 2004

17 Workplace communication

Extra classroom activities

Objective
To talk about different forms of communication in the workplace.

Introduction
In this activity, you are going to plan a new communication policy for your organisation.

What to do
With your partner, first decide how many people work in your organisation. Then:
- put the ideas in order of importance
- decide how much each will cost
- prepare to present your plan to the rest of the class
- tell them what you want.

Input

Here is an email from your boss:

```
To all co-workers,
I would like to improve the way we all communicate
within the organisation. Please would you think about
this and send me your ideas and suggestions by the end
of next week.
I look forward to hearing from you.
With best wishes
The CEO
```

Here are the notes you made after you got the CEO's email:

- A weekend away for everyone – once a year? twice a year? Where?
- An intranet with news – every day? every week?
- A news bulletin to everyone from the CEO every week?
- A monthly newsletter with news about employees?
- Lunch with the CEO for everyone – once a month? once a year?
- A video of company news for all employees – once a month? once every three months?
- Money for sports teams – football? tennis? – so we can all do sport and socialise together more?
- A big Christmas party for everyone – with families? or without?

Which ideas are best?
How much will it all cost?!

18 National dishes

Objective
To talk about different kinds of food.

Introduction
In this activity, you are going to describe foods from different countries.

What to do
With your partner:
1 Decide where each of these dishes comes from.
2 Take it in turns to describe each dish. What are the main ingredients?
3 Can you add national dishes from other countries to these? Can you describe them?

Input

Profiteroles

Moussaka

Caviar

Sweet and sour pork

Hamburger

Pasta

Roast beef and Yorkshire pudding

Curry

Sushi

Goulash

Paella

100 English365 Book 1 © Cambridge University Press 2004

19 Cultural rules and recommendations

Objective
To practise using *should* and *have to*.

Introduction
In this activity, you are going to tell a visitor to your organisation about things he/she should do and things he/she has to do.

What to do
With your partner:
- if you are from the same organisation and/or country, decide what rules and advice to give to a visitor for all of the things below; or
- if you are from different organisations and/or countries, tell each other what rules and advice you would give to a visitor for all of the things below.

Can you think of other important rules or advice?

Use *should* and *have to* as much as possible.

Input

This is the first page of an information booklet which is given to foreign visitors coming to work in your organisation for a short time.

Welcome to our country!
Welcome to our organisation!
We hope you enjoy your stay.

If you have not visited our country before, you should read this booklet because it gives you useful information about how we do things here. It tells you about:

INSIDE THE OFFICE

Clothes to wear at work

Greeting and shaking hands

Calling people by their first or family names

The right time to arrive at the office in the morning

The right time to leave the office in the evening

When meetings start

OUTSIDE THE OFFICE

Talking business in the restaurant

Things you can talk about socially

Things you can't talk about socially

The importance of the family

The importance of religion

20 Computers in your life

Objective
To talk about how you use and how much you use computers.

Introduction
You are going to get information about how other people use their computers.

What to do
Read the questions and write down your own answers.
Ask other students the questions and note their answers.
Report on their computer and Internet use to the rest of the class.

Input

Computer use questionnaire

	You	Partner A	Partner B
1 What kind of computer(s) have you got?			
2 What computer peripherals do you have? (printer, scanner, digital camera, webcam, etc.)			
3 How much time do you spend using a computer every day? At work? At home?			
4 What do you use your computer for?			
5 What do other members of your family use the computer for?			
6 How much time do you spend using the Internet every day? At work? At home?			
7 What do you use the Internet for?			
8 What do other members of your family use the Internet for?			
9 Do you spend too much time on your computer?			
10 Could you live without a computer?			

21 Dream hotel

Objective
To describe a hotel and its services.

Introduction
In this activity, you are going to ask and answer questions about your dream hotel.

What's your dream hotel called?

The first impressions of my dream hotel are wonderful ... it's right on the coast with a view over the sea to the islands. It's very luxurious and very expensive!

What to do
1 Read the report about the Royal Hotel from an international travel magazine.
2 Think about your dream hotel (it can be real or imagined). Use the ideas in the report from a travel magazine below.
3 Think of questions to ask your partner about his/her ideal hotel.
4 Ask your partner questions about his/her dream hotel and note the answers.
5 Tell him/her about yours.
6 Report on your partner's hotel to the rest of the class.

Input

Somewhere for the weekend

Name: The Royal Hotel

Address: Bedford Square, London

First impressions: Beautiful 1905 reception. Luxurious. Expensive.

The bedrooms: 80 rooms. Enormous. Lots of wood.

The beds: Big. Egyptian cotton sheets. Very comfortable.

The bathroom: Enormous bath. Very clean. Modern. Plus jacuzzi.

The restaurant: Three restaurants. Try the Japanese. Delicious fish.

The bar: Two bars. Fantastic cocktails.

The breakfast: Full English breakfast freshly cooked to order.

The lounge: Huge armchairs. Quiet. Papers in six languages.

The view: Nothing special. Ask for a room overlooking the square.

Other facilities: Gym, swimming pool and sauna.

The service: Warm and friendly.

What's nearby: The West End of London – theatres, clubs, museums and shops.

Price: Weekend special offer of €300 per night for bed and breakfast for two. Includes a glass of champagne when you arrive.

Your partner

Name: ....

Address: ....
....

First impressions: ....
....

The bedrooms: ....

The beds: ....

The bathroom: ....

The restaurant: ....

The bar: ....

The breakfast: ....

The lounge: ....

The view: ....

Other facilities: ....

The service: ....

What's nearby: ....

Price: ....
....

22 Number work

Extra classroom activities

Objective
To practise saying numbers in English.

Introduction
In this activity, you are going to:
- look at different kinds of number
- practise saying numbers in English.

What to do
With a partner:
1 Match the written and spoken forms with the type of number in the first column of the table. Write the answers in the right places.
2 Cover up the spoken forms and test each other on how to say the numbers in the second column.
3 Write your own list of numbers and test your partner again.

Input

What it is	How you write it	How you say it
A figure		
A date		
A phone number		
A year		
A price		
An exchange rate		
A percentage		
A time (twelve-hour clock)		
A time (twenty-four hour clock)		

How you write it:
30.10.03 ◆ 123,456 ◆ 7.25 ◆ 99% ◆ 00 44 1904 661683 ◆ €45.70 ◆ $1 = €1.05 ◆ 1789 ◆ 13.55

How you say it:
the thirtieth of October, two thousand and three ◆ twenty-five past seven ◆ ninety-nine per cent seventeen eighty-nine ◆ one hundred and twenty-three thousand, four hundred and fifty-six forty-five euros, seventy cents ◆ double oh, double four, one nine oh four, double six, one six, eight three thirteen fifty-five (five to two) ◆ one point oh five euros to the dollar

104 English365 Book 1 © Cambridge University Press 2004

23 It's my business

Objective
To talk about running a business and business finance.

Introduction
You are going to play the role of a business owner and tell your partner about the business which you manage.

What to do
In this activity, a TV interviewer interviews the owner of a business. One of you will play the role of the interviewer (A), the other the role of the businessperson (B). You will then change roles.
1 Decide with your partner which roles you will take first.
2 Read through the interview and prepare your questions or answers.
3 Now role-play the interview. The interviewer should take notes.
4 Change roles and repeat the exercise.
5 Report back to the class on the financial profile of your partner's company.

Input

A Welcome to Business Daily, TV's most popular business programme. And today we are interviewing ……………… (partner's name) about his/her business. In particular, we are going to ask ……………… (partner's name) about how he/she manages the company's money. So, hello ……………… (partner's name).
B Hello, ……………… (partner's name).
A First of all, what's the name of your company? What's it called?
B It's called ……………… .
A And what is your business? What does your company do?
B We ……………… .
A Interesting. And when did you start the company?
B I started it in ……………… .
A So it's ……………… years old. And how big is it today? What's the turnover?
B The turnover today is ……………… .
A And did you have to borrow money from the bank to start the company?
B Yes, we borrowed ……………… .
A And have you repaid all the money?
B ……………… .
A And are you making a profit now?
B ……………… .
A OK. And what are your major costs?
B Our major costs are ……………… .
A And one final question. If you had ……………… to invest in your business, what would you spend it on?
B I would ……………… .
A OK, thanks very much, ……………… (partner's name). It was very interesting to hear about ……………… (name of company). And now back to the studio.
B Thanks, ……………… (partner's name). It was a pleasure talking to you.

24 Shopping lists

Objective
To practise talking about things you can buy in different shops.

Introduction
In this activity, you are going to talk about different shops and role-play the conversations you can have in them.

What to do
With your partner:
1. Match the sentences with the shops.
2. Think of two or three other things which you can buy in each place.
3. Role-play your own conversation between a customer and an assistant in some of these shops (see the example opposite).
4. Change roles.

> A: Hello. I want to buy a book by Philip Pullman as a present for a child, but I can't remember what it's called.
> B: Northern Lights?
> A: No, I don't think so.
> B: Maybe it's the second one, The Subtle Knife.
> A: Yes, that's right. Have you got a copy?
> B: I'll just look on the computer. I think so …

Input

1. Record store
2. Baker
3. Butcher
4. Post office
5. Jeweller
6. Sports shop
7. Pharmacy
8. Clothes shop
9. Bookshop
10. Travel agency
11. Newsagent

a) Do you have a smaller one? This one's too big for my finger.
b) How much is a letter to Martinique?
c) The *FT*, *The Economist* and *Vogue*, please.
d) I'd like five nights on the Costa del Sol for two in February.
e) Do you have the new *Harry Potter*?
f) A large white and four brown rolls, please.
g) Four steaks and half a kilo of sausages, please.
h) Do you have the Bach Double Violin Concerto?
i) I'd like some new shorts and a pair of size 41 boots.
j) What can you give me for a headache and a bad cold?
k) Can I try another one on? This one's too small.

25 A busy schedule

Objective
To practise talking about future plans using the present continuous tense.

Introduction
Your partner is a very busy person. In this activity, you are going to give him/her information about his/her schedule.

What to do

1 You are the PA (personal assistant) to a senior executive. You have a meeting with him/her in five minutes to present the details of an important three-day trip to the USA which you have organised for him/her. But you have lost his/her diary! You have five minutes to organise your notes before you talk to your boss (your partner). Your notes are opposite but you have to give the dates and times and put the notes in order.

2 How many of these verbs can you use in your presentation?

| attend | come | do | drive | fly | get | go | have | make |
| meet | see | spend | start | talk | | | | |

How many of them can you use in the present continuous to talk about your boss's future plans?
Your partner will score you on the number of times you use this tense.

3 Reverse roles. Which of you used the present continuous most?

Input

Brussels to New York first class

Jogging in Central Park

Presentation to the staff of the American subsidiary, followed by a question and answer session

Tour of the new automated production plant

Check out of your hotel

Meeting with the CEO of your American subsidiary

Presentation to the American Association of Supply Chain Management

New York to Brussels first class

Dinner with press and industry analysts

Meeting with the management committee of your American subsidiary

Lunch with the CEO of your American subsidiary

Drive back to New York

Meeting with the union representatives at your American subsidiary

Squash with the Marketing Director

Meeting with the main shareholders at the Plaza Hotel

Check in to your hotel

Lunch with Bill Smith

Drive to the factory

26 Problems at work

Objective
To use the right language for solving problems between colleagues at work.

Introduction
In this activity, you are going to think about which language is best for dealing with people at work who make problems for you.

What to do
1. Do the quiz on your own.
2. Compare your answers with your partner. Are there some situations where you don't like any of the choices? Or where you like more than one? If you have different answers, discuss them.
3. Report back to the rest of the class.

Input

What do you say when:

1. **a colleague arrives 45 minutes late for a meeting?**
   a You're late again. You must stop doing this.
   b Was the traffic bad again?
   c Please try to be on time for the next meeting.
   d Nice to see you – at last.

2. **two colleagues are talking loudly next to your desk when you are on the phone?**
   a Shut up.
   b Excuse me, I'm on the phone.
   c Please make less noise.
   d Please could you talk more quietly? I'm trying to talk to someone on the phone.

3. **a visitor starts smoking in a non-smoking area of your office?**
   a You can't do that in here.
   b Excuse me, I'm afraid this is a non-smoking area.
   c Please stop smoking immediately.
   d You shouldn't smoke. It's very bad for your health.

4. **a customer complains to you on the telephone?**
   a It's not my fault.
   b I do apologise. I'll make sure it doesn't happen again.
   c I'm sorry. But I can't do anything about it.
   d Please could you call back tomorrow?

5. **your boss asks you to work very late?**
   a I'm sorry I can't.
   b OK. I can stay for a short time.
   c I'm sorry I can't. I have to leave early this evening.
   d How about tomorrow night?

6. **a customer has not paid an invoice?**
   a Can you send some of it?
   b Please could you send us payment as soon as possible?
   c You must pay immediately.
   d If you don't pay, I will contact the legal department.

27 New Year resolutions

Objective
To talk about health and healthy living.

Introduction
In this activity, you are going to talk about rules for a healthy life.

What to do
You and your partner are Jamie's friends. You know that his lifestyle is very unhealthy but you also know that he can't keep 20 resolutions all year. With your partner:
1 Choose the top ten most important resolutions for Jamie.
2 Put them in order of importance from 1 to 10.
3 Report your list to the rest of the class.

Input

Jamie's diary

Dear diary,
It's January 1st. New Year's Day. It was a fantastic party but this morning I feel terrible. I want to be much healthier this year than last year. Here are my New Year resolutions:

1 Give up smoking.
2 Stop drinking alcohol.
3 Stop eating meat.
4 Stop drinking coffee.
5 Drink at least a litre of water every day.
6 Go to bed earlier.
7 Get seven hours' sleep every night.
8 Eat lots of fresh fruit and vegetables.
9 Buy a bicycle.
10 Go for a run every day.
11 Stop driving and start walking to work.
12 Join the local gym club.
13 Go swimming once a week.
14 Stop working so hard.
15 Stop taking work home at the weekend.
16 Lose ten kilos.
17 Stop eating fast food every lunchtime.
18 Stop eating biscuits and chocolate.
19 Join a meditation class.
20 Stop getting stressed about being so unhealthy.

Got to go now – breakfast's ready: sausage and fried eggs – delicious!

28 Executive star

Objective
To practise using the present perfect tense.

Introduction
You are going to find out what a famous business executive has done with his life.

What to do
In this activity, a business journalist interviews the famous business executive, Mark Foster. One of you will play the role of the interviewer, the other the role of the executive. You will then change roles.
1 Decide with your partner which roles you will take first.
2 Read through the notes and prepare your questions or answers.
3 Now role-play the interview. And remember: Mark Foster always speaks in complete sentences.
4 Change roles and repeat the exercise.
5 Report back to the class on the famous executive's life.

Input

Mark Foster is one of Europe's leading executives. He is known especially for his experience with problem companies. He started his career in …

Interview Mark Foster tomorrow!

- How long in business?
- Number of jobs?
- How long in this job?
- Ever made a really big mistake?
- Biggest success?
- When most under pressure?
- Ever sacked someone?
- Most famous person ever met?
- Where travelled on business?
- Best moment?
- Worst moment?
- Ever wanted to do something completely different?
- Ever really late for something?

Other questions?

29 Forecasting the future

Objective
To practise describing increases and decreases.

Introduction
In this activity, you are going to:
- practise using the language of increase and decrease
- forecast different kinds of increase and decrease.

What to do
This activity is in two parts:
1 With a partner, match the eight phrases (1–8) with the graphs (a–h).
2 Ask your partner if he/she thinks there will be increases or decreases in the ten different areas (Personal and Your town or city). Ask for reasons.
3 Report back to the rest of the class on the results of 2.

Input

1 go up a lot
2 increase a little
3 decrease a lot
4 decrease a little
5 stay the same
6 go down a little and then stay the same
7 rise a little and then fall a lot
8 drop a little and then increase a lot

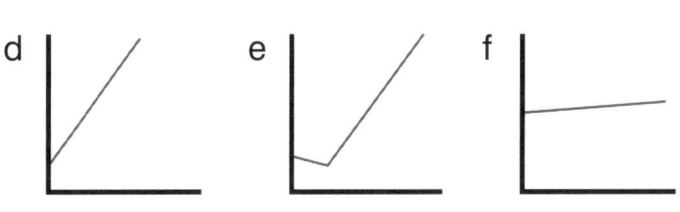

Over the next five years, do you think these will move up or down?

Personal
1 Your salary
2 The hours you work
3 The number of days' holiday you get
4 The money you spend on holidays
5 The money you spend on food
6 The money you spend on entertainment

Your town or city
7 The population of your town or city
8 Traffic in your town or city
9 Crime in your town or city
10 Pollution in your town or city

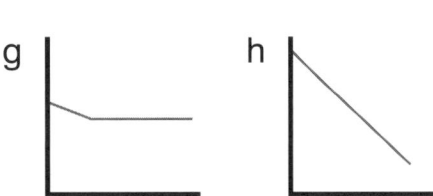

English365 Book 1 © Cambridge University Press 2004

30 Lifestyles

Objective
To talk about different lifestyles.

Introduction
In this activity, you are going to talk about the lifestyle that suits you best.

What to do
1 Read the questionnaire and answer the questions yourself.
2 Ask two or three other students for their answers.
3 Report the results to the rest of the class. What do their answers tell you about the preferred lifestyles of the people in your group?

> I think living in a small town is best. What do you think?

> Well, actually, I think living in a big city is best because there's so much to do.

Input

	You	A	B	C
		Partners		

1 **Location**
  a Living in a big city is best.
  b Living in a small town is best.
  c Living in the country is best.
  d *Your own choice*

2 **Work–life balance**
  a My job is the most important thing in my life.
  b My family is the most important thing in my life.
  c My free time is the most important thing in my life.
  d *Your own choice*

3 **Appearance**
  a My personal appearance is important to me.
  b My personal appearance is important for my job.
  c I'm not very interested in how I look.
  d *Your own choice*

4 **Food**
  a Good food is important to me.
  b Healthy food is important to me.
  c I'm not very interested in food.
  d *Your own choice*

5 **Earning a living**
  a Being self-employed is best.
  b Working for a big organisation is best.
  c Having a private income is best.
  d *Your own choice*

6 **Health and fitness**
  a Lots of exercise every day is best.
  b Some exercise now and again is best.
  c Never taking exercise is best.
  d *Your own choice*

7 **Free time**
  a My idea of a perfect time is partying all night.
  b My idea of a perfect time is lying on a Pacific beach all day.
  c My idea of a perfect time is spending all day climbing a very big hill.
  d *Your own choice*

8 **Age**
  a I would like to be 20 forever.
  b I would like to be 40 forever.
  c I would like to be 60 forever.
  d *Your own choice*

5 Better learning activities

Teacher's notes

Introduction

As well as the 30 photocopiable Extra classroom activities, each linked to one of the units in the Student's Book, there are ten learning-to-learn activities which can be done in parallel with the main course. There is a certain amount of overlap between activities but this should not be a barrier to doing them all since it should serve to emphasise some of the key points. They do not necessarily take up a lot of time but can be critical in encouraging students to think about how they learn and therefore to learn better. Indeed, if any of them question the usefulness of such activities, you might invite them and other students to reflect on what proportion of the course might usefully be given over to this.

The aims of some of these activities are quite sophisticated and the language resources of your students may well be limited. However, as we have said elsewhere, we strongly believe that both students and teachers can say a great deal if they **make the most** of the limited language resources at their mutual disposal.

Since there are ten such activities in the Teacher's Book, you might think about doing one such activity every third lesson or so. Learner training enthusiasts will certainly argue that it is valid to spend 5% to 10% of your time (effectively 5 or 10 minutes of a 90-minute lesson) on this if it leads to higher motivation, retention and effectiveness thereafter.

Procedure
Most of the activities themselves are self-explanatory. They are all designed as pairwork activities and so can be managed in the same way as any others: see the notes on pairwork in the Introduction (page 16). The big difference will lie, however, in the amount of attention you pay to language use and accuracy. As you monitor pairwork communication, your focus should be very much on content rather than form, for here you have the opportunity to learn not only about your students' learning styles but also about the language learning process in general.

Timing
The length of time that it will take to do one of these activities will vary a great deal from class to class. As you get to know each class you teach, you will learn to judge how long you can and should spend on them. Some of the questions are very open-ended and you may wish to delete them from the activity to speed things up: go ahead and do so. Or you may wish to break up activities so that you look at just one or two questions at a time. This is fine too. Sometimes, however, the time you spend on feedback from pairs to the group may be longer than for normal language-focused activities. Learners will learn better if you can help them to extend their repertoire of learning strategies. By encouraging students to share their ideas, you are helping them all to widen this range.

Which language?
If you have a monolingual group, you may even find it appropriate to discuss some of these questions in the students' native language. The only thing to be conscious of is how far the sponsor (the organisation paying for the course) will tolerate this. Hopefully, the organisation will also see the longer-term benefits of improving the learning strategies of its employees.

What to do
- Regardless of the instruction in the *What to do* section of each activity, you can decide whether it's more useful for any given activity for students to report back to the class about themselves or about the person they have been working with.
- You can sometimes provide copies of activities for homework so that students are ready to talk about their answers during the following lesson.

1 Why do you want to learn English?

This activity will provide you with valuable needs analysis information, so you should aim to do it fairly early on in the course – the sooner the better. If possible, it would be useful for you to photocopy students' entries so that they and you can both keep a record of what they indicate.

- Students who already have good opportunities to use English a lot will be at an advantage during the course over those who don't. Therefore those who don't have such opportunities need extra encouragement to consolidate their learning in other ways, for example by working through the Personal Study Book or working on the Follow-up suggestions in the Teacher's notes on the units.
- Degrees of importance and the relative importance of different language areas will also help you to get the balance of input right for each group.

2 Your language learning background

This activity will also give you important information about students' attitudes and aptitude.

- If students already speak more than one language, this *may* signal above average aptitude for languages in general. At least they may be able to reflect on the strategies they used to learn their first L2.
- Experiences of learning languages at school often have an important influence on subsequent expectations about how languages should be learnt and taught, even (or perhaps especially!) when those experiences were not very

positive. People often like talking about their language learning experiences at school. Find out if your students feel they were generally positive or negative ones.
- Question 4 also tells you something about students' linguistic self-esteem. Some people have low linguistic self-esteem, often because of perceptions of failure at school. As with activity 1, it can be useful to make copies of what students record so that you develop insights into which students need more encouragement and support than others.

3 Your level

Do this activity before activity 4 because the same level descriptors are presented again unscrambled. Limit students in this activity to thinking about their current level and what factors determine this. The next activity deals with target levels using the same descriptors.

Check understanding of these key words and phrases:
- 'A level description': One or more sentences saying if a person is good or not so good in a language.
- 'A native speaker of English': A person whose first language is English.
- 'A non-native speaker of English': A person whose first language is not English.
- 'Vocabulary': Words.
- 'Grammar': The rules of a language.
- 'Pronunciation': The way we make the sounds of the language correctly.

Students should first work in pairs to decide the best order for the descriptors and then discuss each other's level. The discussion should raise questions about how to measure competence: through knowledge of grammar? Of vocabulary? Fluency? Accuracy? These are complex issues but it is possible to address them in fairly simple language, such as:
- You speak better than me.
- Maybe, but you know more words than me.

Answers
0 I do not speak English.
1 I have a few words of English.
2 I can only do very simple things in English.
3 I can communicate in English only if people speak very slowly and clearly.
4 I can communicate in English but I make a lot of mistakes and I often have to ask people to speak more slowly.
5 I can work in English but I often have problems understanding and sometimes people have problems understanding me.
6 I can work quite well in English but I know I sometimes make mistakes.
7 I don't have any big problems in English but I sometimes make small mistakes.
8 I speak English almost as well as a lot of native speakers.

4 Fixing targets
- Check understanding of the word *target*.
- Explain to students that setting targets is important in any project – including learning projects – and that fixing long-term goals is the first step in formulating a learning plan.
- It could take some time to work through the questions systematically. Decide whether you want to do this or cut some of the questions as being too specific, or spend some time on this activity now and some more in another lesson.
- It's dangerous to talk about the time it takes to get from one level to another but 40–45 hours (the minimum number of hours of teaching time in *English365* Book 1) could be used as a rough rule of thumb to progress from one level to the next. Ask students first how long they think it takes. Use this opportunity to stress the importance of homework!

5 Making a plan
- Time scale. Listen to what students say about short- and long-term targets when they report back. In fact, it is good to have both a long-term goal and also a, say, weekly learning plan linked to the work they do in the classroom.
- Rewards. This can be presented and treated light-heartedly. But some people do find it very helpful to do this – both short and long term.

6 What makes a good language learner?
- 'I try harder' may seem a little vague but derives from the Avis car hire company customer service slogan 'We try harder' meaning 'We try harder than others to achieve our goals' – a general resolution to make more effort.
- This can be done quite quickly, although you could usefully revisit some of the statements quite often to encourage students to become more engaged in the language learning process. It may be too time-consuming to ask students to decide on a precise ranking from 1 to 10, in which case you may prefer to ask them to simply decide if each statement is very important (V), quite important (Q) or not very important (N).

7 Learning to speak
This can be done quite quickly and semi-humorously but the aim is for some serious points to emerge, for example:
- that good learners will create opportunities to speak and by doing so they gain confidence and practice
- that good learners take risks and are not afraid to make mistakes.

Hopefully students will raise these issues themselves as you discuss their responses to the quiz.

8 Learning to read

Go through the input to make sure students understand all the categories. In particular, this is your opportunity to extol the merits of extensive reading. Tell students about graded readers, in particular the Cambridge University Press series which are original stories. If possible, show them samples of lower level graded readers or encourage them to visit an English language bookshop where they are sold. Regular reading of graded readers is a wonderful way of consolidating language knowledge, developing vocabulary and motivating students to learn more. It can be a central part of any student learning plan. Getting students to make an undertaking to read regularly (see the 'I can promise . . .' section) – even if for just a few minutes a day – can potentially have a major impact on the learning they do and the progress they make.

Ask students to complete the table and then to work in pairs to explain what they have written down and also to work through the other questions.

9 Learning to listen

- Explain any difficult terms, for example *talking book* (an audio cassette or CD of an actor reading a short story or novel, etc.).
- It could be best to get feedback from the class question by question so that students build up a picture of the differences between them.
- Again, you may wish to deal with some of the questions in one lesson and more in another.
- The remark in the introduction was made by Michael Lewis, ELT speaker and author of a number of books, including *The Lexical Approach: The state of ELT and a way forward* (Language Teaching Publications, 1993) and *Teaching Collocation: Further developments in the lexical approach* (Language Teaching Publications, 2000).

10 Learning vocabulary

- You may want to give each student a number of copies of this questionnaire.
- The questions in the questionnaire and following are designed to encourage reflection, so students should not be embarrassed if their ideas are wildly inaccurate or wildly different from each other's. For example, learners at this level often have little idea of the size of their vocabulary and often significantly underestimate, although graded reader syllabi can indicate a passive vocabulary of 700–1,000 or more words. This should come as good news to them!
- There is once again a lot of food for thought in this activity so you may want to split the questions and deal with some in a later lesson.

1 Why do you want to learn English?

Objective
To think about your reasons for learning English.

Name ....

Introduction
In this activity, you are going to think about:
- how you use English
- why you need English
- how important English is to you
- the areas of English (speaking, grammar, etc.) which are important to you.

What to do
1. Answer the questions in 1 to 3 below.
2. Talk about your reasons with a partner.

Input

1 Write figures in the table below:

I use English for:	
Work	%
Travel	%
Pleasure	%
I need English for:	
Work	%
Travel	%
Pleasure	%

2 How important is English to you:
- in your personal life? ☐
- in your professional life? ☐

Use this scale:
3 = very important   2 = quite important   1 = not very important   0 = not at all important

3 Which are the most important areas of English for you to work on?
Number them from 1 to 7 in order of importance:
Speaking ☐
Listening ☐
Reading ☐
Writing ☐
Pronunciation ☐
Vocabulary ☐
Grammar ☐

2 Your language learning background

Objective
To think about your background as a language learner.

Name ....

Introduction
In this activity, you are going to tell your partner about your language learning history.

What to do
1. Look at the questions.
2. Think about the answers.
3. With your partner, ask each other the questions and listen to the answers.
4. Take notes and tell the class about your partner's background.

Input

	You	Your partner
1 Other languages How many languages can you speak? If you can speak another language: • Where did you learn it? • Do you like speaking this language? • Are you good at it?		
2 English When did you last study English? • Is this your first adult course in English? • Did you study English at school? • Were you good at English at school? Why? Why not? • Did you like English at school? • Do you like English now?		
3 Good and bad experiences Tell your partner about a good language learning memory. Tell your partner about a bad language learning memory.		
4 How good are you? How good are you at learning languages? Why do you say this?	Very good ☐ Not very good ☐ Good ☐ Poor ☐ Average ☐	Very good ☐ Not very good ☐ Good ☐ Poor ☐ Average ☐

Better learning activities

3 Your level

Objective
To think about different levels in a language. To decide your level in English.

Name ....

Introduction
Different people have different levels in English. In this activity you will think about:
- different levels of English
- your level
- how you know you are at this level.

What to do
1. With a partner, read the level descriptions and number them in order from weakest (0) to strongest (8). These two have been done for you.
2. Which is your level in English now?
3. Which is your partner's level now?
4. If your level and your partner's level are different, what makes them different?

Input

Levels

☐ [0] I do not speak English.

☐ I can work quite well in English but I know I sometimes make mistakes.

☐ I have a few words of English.

☐ I can communicate in English but I make a lot of mistakes and I often have to ask people to speak more slowly.

☐ I don't have any big problems in English but I sometimes make small mistakes.

☐ I can only do very simple things in English.

☐ I can communicate in English only if people speak very slowly and clearly.

☐ I can work in English but I often have problems understanding and sometimes people have problems understanding me.

☐ [8] I speak English almost as well as a lot of native speakers.

4 Fixing targets

Objective
To think about your targets for learning English.

Name ....

Introduction
Fixing targets is very important for any project. Think about learning English as a project. In this activity, you are going to fix targets for your English.

What to do
Work with a partner to answer questions 1 to 6, then report back to the class.

Input

		You	Your partner
1	What is your general level in English now?		
2	Which general level would you like to have in English?		
3	Which level do you need for your job?		
4	How long do you think it will take for you to reach this level?		
5	Do you need the same level for the different skills? On a scale of 0-8, which level do you need for:	speaking? ☐ ☐ listening? ☐ ☐ reading? ☐ ☐ writing? ☐ ☐	speaking? ☐ ☐ listening? ☐ ☐ reading? ☐ ☐ writing? ☐ ☐
6	What do you want to do in English in one year that you can't do today?		

Levels
0 I do not speak English.
1 I have a few words of English.
2 I can only do very simple things in English.
3 I can communicate in English only if people speak very slowly and clearly.
4 I can communicate in English but I make a lot of mistakes and I often have to ask people to speak more slowly.
5 I can work in English but I often have problems understanding and sometimes people have problems understanding me.
6 I can work quite well in English but I know I sometimes make mistakes.
7 I don't have any big problems in English but I sometimes make small mistakes.
8 I speak English almost as well as a lot of native speakers.

5 Making a plan

Better learning activities

Objective
To make a plan for learning English.

Name ....

Introduction
In this activity, you are going to think about how to plan your English learning. The questions in the activity will help you decide your plan.

What to do
1. Think about your answers and write them down.
2. Discuss your answers with a partner.
3. Report your work to the rest of the class.

Input

TIME SCALE
Is it better to have:
- short-term targets? ☐   Why? ....
- long-term targets? ☐   Why? ....
- both? ☐   Why? ....

Is your plan for:
3 months? ☐   6 months? ☐   9 months? ☐   1 year? ☐

TIME
'Doing a little English every day is better than doing a lot once a week.' Do you agree? Yes ☐   No ☐
How much time can you give to English each day? Be realistic.
Minutes: 5 ☐   10 ☐   15 ☐   20 ☐   30 ☐   40 ☐   50 ☐   60 ☐
How many days a week do you plan to study English?
Days: 1 ☐   2 ☐   3 ☐   4 ☐   5 ☐   6 ☐   7 ☐

TARGETS
Write down your three main long-term targets for learning English. Be clear. Be specific.
1 ....
2 ....
3 ....

REWARDS
Give yourself a prize when you reach each of your targets! What will they be?
1 ....
2 ....
3 ....

6 What makes a good language learner?

Name ....

Better learning activities

Objective
To think about what makes a good language learner. To think about ways to become a better language learner yourself.

Introduction
In this activity, you are going to:
- look at things which language learners say
- say how useful these are
- say which ones you want to try.

What to do
Work with a partner.
1 Decide if these sentences are all things which good language learners say.
2 Put them in order from most useful (10) to least useful (1).
3 Say which ones you try or will try in your own learning.

Input

a ☐ I feel positive about learning English.

b ☐ I feel positive about English and about people who speak English.

c ☐ I try harder.

d ☐ I fix targets.

e ☐ I have a learning plan.

f ☐ I learn from my mistakes.

g ☐ I think about what I learn.

h ☐ I think about how I learn.

i ☐ I speak English as much as I can.

j ☐ I don't worry about making mistakes.

English365 Book 1 © Cambridge University Press 2004 **121**

7 Learning to speak

Objective
To think about what language learners do to be good speakers.

Name ....

Introduction
In this activity, you are going to do a quiz to see how much you try to speak English when you have the chance.

What to do
Work with a partner and read the questions.
1 Decide what you would do in each case.
2 Decide what the best thing to do is in each case.
3 How can you start doing the best thing if you don't already do it?

Input

1 You arrive at work to find an English-speaking visitor in reception. The receptionist does not speak English. Do you:
  a walk past?
  b stop and help?
  c find someone who can help?

2 You are on holiday. You can go shopping in the local market (where you have to speak English) or at the supermarket (where you don't). Do you:
  a shop in the market?
  b shop in the supermarket?
  c go hungry?

3 The phone rings in your office. You know your colleague is waiting for a call from the USA but he/she is not there. Do you:
  a answer the phone?
  b ask a colleague to answer?
  c quickly leave the office?

4 You go to your company restaurant. Your colleague is having lunch with an English-speaking guest. Do you:
  a have lunch with them and join the conversation?
  b have lunch with them but only listen?
  c sit at another table?

5 A visitor to your town or city asks you for help in the street. Do you say:
  a 'I'm sorry, I don't speak English.'
  b 'I'm sorry, I'm a visitor here myself.'
  c 'Welcome to our town. What can I do to help?'

8 Learning to read

Objective
To think about the importance of reading as a way of learning English.

Name ....

Introduction
In this activity, you are going to think about:
- what you can read in English and
- how much you can read as part of your learning plan.

What to do
1. Look at the different kinds of reading, then fill in the table.
2. Tell your partner what you wrote and discuss these questions:
   - Do you like reading in your own language? What do you like reading?
   - Can you think of any more kinds of reading?
   - Is reading a good way to learn English?

Input

The Internet

Emails

Graded readers

Books

Business and technical reports

Newspapers

General interest magazines

Special interest magazines

Magazines for language learners

Websites for language learners

COMICS AND COMIC BOOKS

Children's books

Parallel translation books

The three most interesting kinds of reading for me are:

1 ....

2 ....

3 ....

I can promise to read in English for .... minutes a day / week / month.

Better learning activities

9 Learning to listen

Better learning activities

Objective
To think about listening and about ways to improve your listening.

Name ....

Introduction
A wise English teacher once said: 'You don't learn to talk by talking. You learn to talk by listening.' In this activity, you are going to think about the importance of listening and about how you can learn to listen better.

What to do
Work with a partner and ask and answer the questions below. What kind of listener is your partner? How is he/she different from you?

Input

Food for thought	You	Your partner
Are you a good listener in your own language?		
What makes a good listener?		
How easy or difficult is listening for you in English?		
What makes listening in English difficult?		
Do you prefer to start learning by talking or by listening?		
Is it best to try and get a general idea of what someone is saying to you in English or to understand every word?		
What do you like listening to best in English? • Videos / DVDs (with or without subtitles?) • The radio • Audio cassettes / CDs for English learners • Other people: native speakers or non-native speakers of English • Talking books	☐ ☐ ☐ ☐ ☐	☐ ☐ ☐ ☐ ☐

124 English365 Book 1 © Cambridge University Press 2004

10 Learning vocabulary

Objective
To think about learning vocabulary – how to learn more and learn it better.

Name ....

Introduction
In this activity, you are going to do a class survey to find out about other students' vocabulary and how they learn new words.

What to do
To do the survey, talk to as many members of your class as you can.
Then prepare answers to the questions 1 to 4 before you report back to the class and to your teacher.

Input

Class questionnaire

1 How many words do you know in English?
2 What is your vocabulary learning target? (per day? per week? per month?)
3 How do you organise your vocabulary notebook?
4 How do you learn new words?

1 Who knows the most words in English? ....
2 Who has the highest vocabulary learning target? ....
3 Notebooks:
  - How many people in the class do/don't have a vocabulary notebook? ....
  - How many organise it in the same way as you? ....
  - What's the most popular way to organise it? ....
  - What do you think is the best way? ....

4 Learning new words:
  - How many people learn words in the same way as you? ....
  - What is the most popular way to learn new words? ....
  - What does it mean to learn a word? ....

Teacher's diary

Date	Class
Unit objectives	

How do I rate the lesson?

1 Terrible ☐   2 Not very good ☐   3 Satisfactory ☐   4 Good ☐   5 Excellent ☐

What went well?

What went less well?

Did I try anything new?

What should I think about for next time?

Anything memorable?